The
VIRGO PATH
YOUR DAILY 2025 HOROSCOPE GUIDE

AMANDA M CLARKE

Welcome to The Virgo Path: Your Daily 2025 Horoscope Guide. This book is designed to provide Virgo readers with daily astrological insights, offering guidance, inspiration, and cosmic wisdom for each day of the year. Whether you're seeking clarity on love, career, or personal growth, these horoscopes will help you navigate the year ahead with mindfulness and intention. Use this guide to reflect, set positive intentions, and align with the universe's energy as you walk your unique path in 2025.

Copyright © 2024 by Koru Lifestylist

All rights reserved. All content, materials, and intellectual property in this book or any other platform owned by Koru Lifestylist are protected by copyright laws. This includes text, images, graphics, videos, audio, software, and any other form of content that may be produced by Koru Lifestylist.

No part of this content may be reproduced, distributed, or transmitted in any form or by any means without the prior written permission of Koru Lifestylist. This means that you cannot copy, reproduce, or use any of the content in this book for commercial or personal purposes without the express written consent of Koru Lifestylist.

Unauthorized use of any copyrighted material owned by Koru Lifestylist may result in legal action being taken against you. Koru Lifestylist reserves the right to pursue all available legal remedies against any individual or entity found to be infringing on its copyright.

In summary, Koru Lifestylist © 2024 holds exclusive rights to all the content produced by it, and any unauthorized use of such content will result in legal action.

Disclaimer: The Virgo Path: Your daily 2025 horoscope guide book provides information on astrological readings and intuitive interpretations, it is not intended as a substitute for professional advice, diagnosis, or treatment. The information contained in this book is provided for educational and entertainment purposes only and is not meant to be taken as specific advice for individual circumstances. The author and publisher make no representations or warranties with respect to the accuracy or completeness of the contents of this book and specifically disclaim any implied warranties of merchantability or fitness for a particular purpose. The reader should always consult with a licensed professional for any specific concerns or questions. The author and publisher shall not be liable for any loss or damage caused or alleged to have been caused, directly or indirectly, by the information contained in this book. The use of this book is at the reader's sole risk

VIRGO
August 23 – September 22

2025
Overview

Virgo in 2025 Overview

Virgo, 2025 is a year of growth, transformation, and newfound clarity for you. You'll feel an increased focus on personal development, with opportunities to realign with your true goals. The year encourages you to evaluate your routines, relationships, and career choices, making thoughtful changes where needed. With careful planning, your practical nature will shine, helping you manifest your dreams into reality.

Expect breakthroughs in your professional life, as dedication pays off, bringing recognition and success. In relationships, deeper connections emerge, offering fulfillment and emotional security. Embrace change, trust your instincts, and keep moving forward—2025 will be a year of personal empowerment and balance.

Virgo in 2025
Love and Relationships

Virgo, 2025 is a year of emotional growth and deeper connections in your love life. If you're in a relationship, expect opportunities to strengthen your bond through open communication and mutual understanding. Any lingering issues from the past may surface early in the year, but with patience and honesty, you'll overcome them, emerging stronger as a couple.

For single Virgos, 2025 brings a fresh start. New romantic opportunities may come from unexpected places, and you'll feel more confident in pursuing what you truly desire in a partner. This year encourages you to set clear boundaries and trust your instincts when navigating new relationships.

Whether in a relationship or single, this is a year for nurturing emotional intimacy and building connections that align with your values.

Virgo in 2025
Career

Virgo, 2025 is a powerful year for your career, as hard work and dedication start to bear fruit. This year, your analytical skills and attention to detail will help you stand out in professional settings, leading to recognition, advancement, or new opportunities. Whether you're seeking a promotion, career change, or expanding your own business, your practical nature and persistence will guide you to success.

The first half of the year may involve restructuring your goals and refining your approach, but by mid-year, you'll see clear progress. New projects or responsibilities may emerge, requiring adaptability and leadership, but trust in your abilities to rise to the occasion. Networking will also play a crucial role, so don't hesitate to expand your connections.

Overall, 2025 is a year to build, plan, and elevate your career. Stay focused on long-term goals, and the rewards will follow.

Virgo in 2025
Wealth

Virgo, 2025 brings promising developments in your financial life, thanks to your careful planning and disciplined approach. This year is all about building stability and setting the groundwork for long-term financial security. Whether through investments, savings, or smart budgeting, your practical nature will help you grow your wealth steadily.

Opportunities for increased income may arise, particularly mid-year, as your hard work in your career begins to pay off. However, it's important to avoid impulsive spending. Instead, focus on saving and investing wisely. Real estate or long-term investments could be particularly favorable this year.

Unexpected expenses may pop up in the latter half of the year, but with your cautious nature, you'll be prepared to handle them without much disruption. Keep reviewing your financial goals, and 2025 will be a year of steady financial growth and security.

Virgo in 2025
Health

Virgo, 2025 encourages you to prioritize your well-being, both physically and mentally. With your tendency to focus on productivity and responsibility, it's essential to make time for self-care this year. The first half of 2025 may bring a renewed focus on creating healthier routines, such as improving your diet, fitness, or sleep habits. Small, consistent changes will have lasting benefits.

Mental health will also be a key focus, as stress from career and personal life may accumulate. Finding balance through mindfulness practices like yoga, meditation, or simply taking breaks will be vital to maintaining mental clarity.

Mid-year, you might feel energized, making it a great time to engage in new fitness activities or explore outdoor adventures. However, don't push yourself too hard—listen to your body and give yourself the rest you need.

Overall, 2025 is about creating sustainable health habits and achieving a harmonious balance between body and mind.

Virgo in 2025
Study

Virgo, 2025 is a year of intellectual growth and focus, making it an excellent time for pursuing studies or enhancing your skills. Whether you're in formal education or learning something new to advance your career, your natural curiosity and disciplined approach will help you excel.

The first half of the year may require extra focus on time management, as balancing study with other responsibilities could be challenging. However, your strong organizational skills will help you stay on track and achieve your goals.

Mid-year, new opportunities for learning may arise, such as courses, certifications, or mentorship programs that align with your long-term ambitions. Embrace these opportunities, as they can set you up for future success.

Overall, 2025 is a year to broaden your knowledge, sharpen your skills, and stay open to new learning experiences that will contribute to your personal and professional growth.

*To my dearest Virgo friend,
Vonny Vonners,
Your strength, wisdom, and
unwavering support have been a
guiding light in my life.*

*This book is dedicated to you, with
love and gratitude for all the ways you
inspire me.*

*May the stars continue to shine as
brightly for you as you do for those
around you.*

VIRGO
Daily Horoscope 2025

January 2025

Virgo

01 January 2025

Today Dear Virgo, you may feel the urge to express your thoughts more clearly. Conversations that have been lingering in the back of your mind can now be addressed with confidence. Be mindful of your tone and approach, as today's energy supports open dialogue and understanding. Relationships, both personal and professional, will benefit from your honesty. Don't shy away from tough subjects. Clarity is your friend today, helping to resolve misunderstandings. Allow yourself to be vulnerable and trust that speaking from the heart will lead to positive outcomes.

Affirmation & Gratitude

"I communicate clearly and compassionately, trusting that honesty strengthens my connections."

Virgo
02 January 2025

Today Dear Virgo, the energy of the day supports structure and organization. You might feel a strong need to tidy up your physical environment or streamline your daily schedule. Take advantage of this momentum to declutter and create space, both mentally and physically. Efficiency will be your key today, and by the end of the day, you'll feel lighter and more in control. Small changes can lead to big results, so don't underestimate the power of a little tidying and planning.

Affirmation & Gratitude

"I create order in my life, knowing that organization leads to peace and clarity."

Virgo

03 January 2025

Today Dear Virgo, introspection is the theme. The day invites you to look inward and reflect on your goals, emotions, and relationships. Spend some time in quiet contemplation, and listen to your inner voice. Answers you seek may be found in stillness. It's a great day for journaling, meditation, or simply sitting in nature to clear your mind. Let go of external noise and tune in to what your heart truly desires. This introspective time will help guide your next steps with confidence and clarity.

Affirmation & Gratitude

"I trust my inner wisdom and embrace moments of stillness for reflection and growth."

Virgo
04 January 2025

Today Dear Virgo, practical matters take center stage. Your sharp mind and attention to detail will serve you well as you tackle tasks that require focus and precision. Whether it's at work or in personal projects, you'll find satisfaction in problem-solving and efficiency. Don't be afraid to roll up your sleeves and get things done. Your efforts will not go unnoticed, and you'll feel accomplished by the day's end. Keep your focus steady and enjoy the feeling of productivity.

Affirmation & Gratitude

"I am capable of handling any task with focus and confidence, trusting in my abilities."

Virgo
05 January 2025

Today Dear Virgo, your social life may take a pleasant turn. Friends and loved ones may seek your company, and it's a great day to connect with others. Don't hesitate to initiate conversations or reach out to someone you've been thinking of. Your energy is warm and inviting today, which makes it easier to strengthen bonds. Sharing your time and laughter with those who matter most will uplift your spirits. Embrace the power of connection and let it nourish your heart.

Affirmation & Gratitude

"I cherish the connections in my life, knowing they bring joy and meaning to my journey."

Virgo

06 January 2025

Today Dear Virgo, self-care is calling your name. You've been working hard, and now it's time to recharge. Whether through physical rest, pampering, or simply taking a mental break, give yourself permission to slow down. You deserve to nurture your body and soul, and today's energy supports healing and rejuvenation. Tune in to your needs and honor them fully. A little rest will go a long way in restoring your energy and vitality.

Affirmation & Gratitude

"I honor my body and mind, giving myself the rest and care I deserve to feel renewed."

Virgo
07 January 2025

Today Dear Virgo, your analytical mind is in full swing. Problem-solving comes naturally today, and you may find yourself focusing on tasks that require precision and careful attention. Whether it's at work, home, or even in your personal relationships, your ability to see the finer details will be a valuable asset. Don't rush through anything; instead, take your time to ensure things are done correctly. This careful approach will lead to success and a sense of accomplishment by the day's end.

Affirmation & Gratitude

"I trust in my ability to solve problems and handle details with focus and care."

♍ Virgo
08 January 2025

Today Dear Virgo, creativity flows through you, sparking new ideas and possibilities. Today's energy invites you to explore your creative side, whether it's through art, writing, or a personal project. Don't be afraid to think outside the box or try something new. Your imagination is a powerful tool, and when you give it space to flourish, it can lead to exciting breakthroughs. Take a break from the usual routine and allow your creative spirit to take the lead.

Affirmation & Gratitude

"I embrace my creativity, allowing inspiration to flow freely and guide me toward new possibilities."

Virgo

09 January 2025

Today Dear Virgo, change is in the air, and you may feel a pull toward new experiences or shifts in your routine. While change can be unsettling at times, today's energy encourages you to welcome it with open arms. Trust that any shifts happening now are leading you to where you need to be. Be flexible and adaptable, and you'll find that change can bring new opportunities and growth.

Affirmation & Gratitude

"I welcome change with grace, trusting that it leads to new opportunities and growth."

Virgo
10 January 2025

Today Dear Virgo, relationships are highlighted. It's a great day to nurture your connections with others, especially those that have been strained or distant. Open your heart and engage in meaningful conversations. Your ability to listen and offer support will strengthen your bonds. Remember that relationships are a two-way street, so be sure to give as much as you receive. This day can bring healing and deeper understanding if you approach it with empathy and care.

Affirmation & Gratitude

"I nurture my relationships with love, understanding, and compassion, knowing they bring richness to my life."

Virgo

11 January 2025

Today Dear Virgo, your drive for success is strong, and you're ready to make progress on long-term goals. Focus on the steps you need to take and avoid distractions. You may feel a boost of motivation to tackle projects that have been on hold. Trust your capabilities and take steady, calculated actions. Your efforts will start to pay off soon, so keep your eyes on the prize and maintain your momentum. Use today's energy to plan for the future with clarity and purpose.

Affirmation & Gratitude

"I am focused and determined, taking steps toward my goals with confidence and clarity."

Virgo
12 January 2025

Today Dear Virgo, it's a perfect day to review your financial situation or plan for future investments. Whether it's budgeting, saving, or making long-term financial decisions, today's energy supports practicality and foresight. Stay grounded in your approach and make decisions that align with your long-term goals. Avoid impulsive purchases or risky investments; instead, trust your analytical nature to guide you toward smart choices. Financial stability is within reach if you stay disciplined.

Affirmation & Gratitude

"I manage my finances with care and wisdom, trusting that each choice builds a secure future."

Virgo
13 January 2025

Today Dear Virgo, your meticulous nature will shine through in everything you do. You'll find satisfaction in organizing, planning, and paying attention to the finer details of your day. Whether it's at work or in your personal life, this attention to detail will help you accomplish tasks with precision. Don't rush through anything; take your time to ensure quality in your efforts. Your hard work will not go unnoticed, and you'll feel a sense of accomplishment by the end of the day.

Affirmation & Gratitude

"I take pride in my attention to detail, knowing it leads to success and accomplishment."

Virgo
14 January 2025

Today Dear Virgo, you may feel the need for solitude and introspection. It's a day to retreat from the busyness of life and reconnect with yourself. Take some quiet time to reflect on your goals, emotions, and personal growth. Journaling or meditation will be especially helpful today. Use this time to clear your mind and regain clarity on any areas of confusion. Your inner wisdom is strong, and by the end of the day, you'll feel more centered and at peace.

Affirmation & Gratitude

"I embrace moments of solitude, allowing myself to reflect and gain clarity on my path forward."

Virgo
15 January 2025

Today Dear Virgo, energy is high, and you're ready to tackle any challenges that come your way. Use this boost of motivation to make progress on your projects and responsibilities. Your confidence and drive will help you push through obstacles with ease. This is a great day to take initiative and start something new. Whether at work or in your personal life, trust your instincts and go after what you want. Success is within reach if you stay focused.

Affirmation & Gratitude

"I am energized and confident, ready to take action and make progress toward my goals."

Virgo
16 January 2025

Today Dear Virgo, communication is key. Whether at work, home, or with friends, your words will carry weight. Take the time to clearly express your thoughts and feelings. Today is a great day to resolve misunderstandings or have important conversations. Your ability to listen and speak with clarity will lead to positive outcomes. Don't shy away from addressing difficult topics—honest and open communication will strengthen your relationships and bring understanding.

Affirmation & Gratitude

"I communicate openly and honestly, trusting that clarity leads to stronger and healthier connections."

# Virgo
17 January 2025

Today Dear Virgo, you may find yourself feeling more sensitive than usual. It's important to protect your energy and avoid environments that feel overwhelming. Focus on self-care and emotional balance today. Surround yourself with supportive people who uplift your spirits. If you need to take a step back from social obligations, don't hesitate to do so. Prioritize your emotional well-being, and you'll feel recharged and ready to face the world again soon.

Affirmation & Gratitude

"I honor my emotional well-being, giving myself the space and care I need to feel balanced."

Virgo

18 January 2025

Today Dear Virgo, it's a day to focus on your relationships. Whether romantic, familial, or friendships, give your connections the attention they deserve. Acts of kindness and support will go a long way in strengthening your bonds. If someone close to you needs a helping hand or a listening ear, be there for them. The love and care you give today will create a positive ripple effect in your life and theirs.

Affirmation & Gratitude

"I nurture my relationships with love and compassion, knowing that strong connections bring joy and fulfillment."

♍ Virgo

19 January 2025

Today Dear Virgo, curiosity and learning are at the forefront. You may feel a strong desire to expand your knowledge or dive deeper into a subject that interests you. Whether it's through reading, taking a course, or exploring new ideas, today is a perfect day to feed your mind. Intellectual growth will bring you a sense of satisfaction and help you see the world from a new perspective. Trust that the knowledge you gain today will serve you well in the future.

Affirmation & Gratitude

"I am grateful for my curiosity and the joy of learning new things every day."

Virgo
20 January 2025

Today Dear Virgo, balance is essential. You may be juggling multiple responsibilities, but it's important to find harmony between work and personal life. Don't let yourself get overwhelmed by trying to do everything at once. Prioritize what's most important and allow yourself time to relax and recharge. By maintaining balance, you'll be more productive and less stressed. Focus on creating a daily routine that supports your well-being and allows for both work and play.

Affirmation & Gratitude

"I create balance in my life, knowing that harmony leads to peace and fulfillment."

Virgo
21 January 2025

Today Dear Virgo, it's time to tie up loose ends. Any projects or commitments that have been lingering should be completed today. The energy is perfect for bringing things to a close and clearing the path for new opportunities. Don't leave anything unfinished. Once you've wrapped up these tasks, you'll feel a sense of relief and accomplishment, ready to move forward with a clean slate.

Affirmation & Gratitude

"I complete what I've started, creating space for new opportunities and growth in my life."

Virgo
22 January 2025

Today Dear Virgo, collaboration is highlighted. Working with others will bring greater success than going it alone. Whether at work or in personal projects, seek out partnerships and collaborations that allow everyone to contribute their strengths. Don't hesitate to share your ideas and offer support to others. Together, you can achieve more than you would on your own. Today is a reminder that teamwork makes the dream work.

Affirmation & Gratitude

"I am grateful for the power of teamwork and the shared success it brings."

Virgo

23 January 2025

Today Dear Virgo, details matter. Whether you're working on a big project or simply managing daily tasks, your attention to detail will make a significant difference. Take the time to double-check your work, and don't rush through anything. Your meticulous approach will ensure success, and others will appreciate your thoroughness. Today's energy supports quality over quantity, so focus on doing things right the first time.

Affirmation & Gratitude

"I take pride in my attention to detail, knowing it leads to high-quality results and success."

Virgo

24 January 2025

Today Dear Virgo, a sense of renewal fills the air. It's time to let go of old habits, situations, or mindsets that no longer serve you. Embrace the fresh energy surrounding you and be open to new possibilities. Today is a great day to set new intentions and create positive changes in your life. Trust that by releasing the old, you make space for the new and exciting opportunities ahead.

Affirmation & Gratitude

"I release what no longer serves me and welcome new energy and opportunities into my life."

Virgo
25 January 2025

Today Dear Virgo, your intuition is heightened. Trust your gut instincts today, especially when making decisions. Your inner voice is guiding you toward the right path, and by listening to it, you'll avoid unnecessary complications. Whether it's a personal or professional matter, follow your heart and trust that you know what's best. You have all the wisdom you need within you.

Affirmation & Gratitude

"I trust my intuition and allow it to guide me toward my highest good and truth."

Virgo
26 January 2025

Today Dear Virgo, family and loved ones may take center stage. It's a perfect day to spend quality time with those closest to you. Whether it's a simple gathering or a meaningful conversation, focus on strengthening your family bonds. Your presence and attention will mean a lot to your loved ones, and in return, you'll feel supported and appreciated.

Affirmation & Gratitude

"I am grateful for the love and support of my family and cherish every moment we share together."

Virgo

27 January 2025

Today Dear Virgo, expect some unexpected changes. Life may throw a curveball your way, but stay flexible and adaptable. Change can bring new opportunities and growth, so don't resist it. Trust that whatever happens today is leading you to where you need to be. Stay open-minded and embrace the unknown with curiosity and courage.

Affirmation & Gratitude

"I embrace change with an open heart, knowing it brings growth and new possibilities into my life."

 Virgo
28 January 2025

Today Dear Virgo, it's a day for setting intentions and mapping out your future goals. Take time to reflect on what you want to achieve in the coming months and create a plan to make it happen. Focus on long-term success and think about the steps you need to take to get there. Setting clear intentions today will help you manifest your desires in the future.

Affirmation & Gratitude

"I set clear intentions for my future, knowing that each step I take brings me closer to my dreams."

Virgo

29 January 2025

Today Dear Virgo, take a moment to appreciate all you've accomplished. You've worked hard, and now it's time to enjoy the fruits of your labor. Celebrate your successes, both big and small, and recognize how far you've come. Gratitude will amplify your abundance, so take a moment to express appreciation for all the good in your life.

Affirmation & Gratitude

"I celebrate my accomplishments and am grateful for the abundance and success in my life."

♍ Virgo
30 January 2025

Today Dear Virgo, your creativity is flowing, and today is the perfect day to let your imagination take the lead. Whether you're working on a creative project or solving a problem, allow yourself to think outside the box. Your innovative ideas will bring fresh solutions and inspiration. Don't be afraid to take risks and explore new possibilities.

Affirmation & Gratitude

"I embrace my creative spirit and allow it to inspire new ideas and possibilities in my life."

Virgo
31 January 2025

Today Dear Virgo, the month ends on a high note. You may receive recognition or a breakthrough in a project you've been working on. Celebrate your achievements and trust that your hard work is paying off. You've earned the success and praise coming your way, so be open to receiving it. Trust in your talents and abilities as you move forward.

Affirmation & Gratitude

"I am open to receiving recognition and celebrate the success I have worked hard to achieve."

February 2025

Virgo
01 February 2025

Today Dear Virgo, you may feel a burst of creative energy. Let your imagination run wild and explore new ideas. Whether it's through art, writing, or problem-solving, your creativity will shine today. Don't hold back—this is the perfect time to express yourself freely. Your innovative approach will attract positive attention and open doors to new opportunities. Trust your instincts and let your creativity flow without judgment. You'll be amazed by what you can accomplish when you let your imagination take the lead.

Affirmation & Gratitude

"I embrace my creativity and let my imagination guide me toward new possibilities."

♍ Virgo
02 February 2025

Today Dear Virgo, your attention turns to relationships. It's a good day to connect deeply with loved ones and nurture your bonds. Whether it's through meaningful conversations or acts of kindness, your efforts will strengthen the relationships that matter most to you. If there have been any misunderstandings, today is the perfect time to clear the air and bring healing to any strained connections. Approach others with compassion and openness, and you'll find that love and understanding flow easily.

Affirmation & Gratitude

"I nurture my relationships with love and compassion, strengthening the bonds that bring joy to my life."

Virgo
03 February 2025

Today Dear Virgo, your practical nature comes to the forefront. You'll find satisfaction in organizing and bringing structure to your day. Whether it's tidying up your workspace or streamlining your daily tasks, today's energy supports efficiency and productivity. Take the time to plan and prioritize, and you'll feel a sense of accomplishment by the end of the day. Don't hesitate to tackle any lingering tasks that require your attention. Your ability to focus and manage details will lead to success.

Affirmation & Gratitude

"I bring order and structure to my life, knowing that organization leads to peace and productivity."

Virgo
04 February 2025

Today Dear Virgo, it's a day for introspection and reflection. Take some quiet time to connect with your inner self and reflect on your personal journey. Journaling, meditation, or simply spending time in nature will help you gain clarity on your emotions and goals. This introspective time will provide valuable insights into your next steps. Don't rush through the day—allow yourself the space to sit with your thoughts and feelings. You'll emerge with a deeper understanding of yourself and your path forward.

Affirmation & Gratitude

"I honor moments of introspection, allowing myself the space to reflect and grow."

Virgo

05 February 2025

Today Dear Virgo, your energy is focused on problem-solving. Whether at work or in your personal life, you'll have a clear vision of how to approach challenges. Use your analytical mind to break down complex issues into manageable steps, and you'll find solutions that benefit everyone involved. Today's energy supports practical thinking and attention to detail, so don't shy away from tackling tough tasks. Your efforts will lead to positive outcomes and progress.

Affirmation & Gratitude

"I trust my problem-solving abilities and approach challenges with clarity and focus."

Virgo
06 February 2025

Today Dear Virgo, self-care is a priority. You may feel the need to rest and recharge after a busy period. Take time to focus on your well-being, whether through physical rest, emotional nourishment, or simply slowing down. Listen to your body and honor its needs. Today's energy supports healing and renewal, so don't hesitate to take a break from the hustle and bustle. You'll return to your responsibilities feeling refreshed and ready to tackle what's ahead.

Affirmation & Gratitude

"I honor my body's need for rest and renewal, allowing myself to recharge and feel rejuvenated."

Virgo
07 February 2025

Today Dear Virgo, communication is key. Whether in your personal or professional life, your ability to express yourself clearly and thoughtfully will lead to positive results. Today's energy supports honest and open conversations, so don't be afraid to share your thoughts and feelings. You'll find that others are receptive to your words, and any misunderstandings can be resolved with ease. Be a good listener as well, as valuable insights can come from truly hearing others' perspectives.

Affirmation & Gratitude

"I communicate with clarity and openness, trusting that honest conversations lead to understanding and connection."

Virgo
08 February 2025

Today Dear Virgo, it's a great day for learning and expanding your knowledge. You may feel a strong desire to explore new subjects or dive deeper into a topic that interests you. Whether it's through reading, taking a course, or simply having intellectual conversations, today's energy supports growth and curiosity. Allow yourself to be a student of life, and you'll find joy in learning new things. The knowledge you gain today will serve you well in the future.

Affirmation & Gratitude

"I am grateful for my curiosity and the joy of learning and expanding my mind."

Virgo
09 February 2025

Today Dear Virgo, balance is the theme. It's important to find harmony between work and relaxation. You may have been pushing yourself hard recently, but today's energy invites you to slow down and restore balance. Focus on creating a routine that allows for both productivity and self-care. When you achieve balance, you'll find that you're more effective and less stressed. Prioritize your well-being as much as your responsibilities, and you'll feel more centered.

Affirmation & Gratitude

"I create balance in my life, knowing that harmony leads to peace and fulfillment."

Virgo
10 February 2025

Today Dear Virgo, it's time to complete unfinished tasks and tie up loose ends. Today's energy supports closure, so take this opportunity to finish any projects or commitments that have been lingering. By wrapping things up, you'll create space for new opportunities and experiences. Don't procrastinate—embrace the sense of accomplishment that comes with completing what you've started. You'll feel a sense of relief and readiness for the next chapter.

Affirmation & Gratitude

"I complete what I've started, creating space for new opportunities and growth."

Virgo
11 February 2025

Today Dear Virgo, teamwork is highlighted. Whether you're collaborating with colleagues or working on a group project, today's energy supports cooperation and shared success. Embrace the idea that two heads are better than one, and be open to working closely with others. Your ability to contribute your strengths to the group will lead to greater achievements than you could accomplish alone. Don't hesitate to offer support or ask for help when needed.

Affirmation & Gratitude

"I am grateful for the power of teamwork and the shared success it brings."

 Virgo
12 February 2025

Today Dear Virgo, you'll feel a surge of motivation and energy. It's a great day to start something new or make progress on a project that's been on your mind. Whether it's personal or professional, your enthusiasm and determination will help you move forward with confidence. Use this boost of energy to take bold actions and pursue your goals. Success is within reach if you stay focused and committed.

Affirmation & Gratitude

"I am energized and motivated, ready to take bold actions toward my goals with confidence."

Virgo
13 February 2025

Today Dear Virgo, details matter. Your meticulous nature will serve you well as you focus on tasks that require precision and careful attention. Whether it's at work or in your personal life, your ability to manage the finer details will lead to success. Take your time to ensure that everything is done correctly, and don't rush through any important tasks. Your thoroughness will be appreciated, and you'll feel a sense of accomplishment by the day's end.

Affirmation & Gratitude

"I take pride in my attention to detail, knowing that it leads to success and satisfaction."

Virgo
14 February 2025

Today Dear Virgo, love and relationships are in focus. Whether you're single or in a partnership, today's energy supports romance, connection, and deepening bonds. Spend quality time with someone you care about and express your love openly. If you've been wanting to have a heartfelt conversation, today is the perfect day to share your feelings. Your vulnerability will strengthen your relationships and bring you closer to those you cherish.

Affirmation & Gratitude

"I nurture love and connection in my life, knowing that strong relationships bring joy and fulfillment."

 Virgo
15 February 2025

Today Dear Virgo, your intuition is heightened, and you may find that your gut feelings are guiding you in the right direction. Trust your instincts today, especially when making decisions. Your inner wisdom is strong, and by listening to it, you'll avoid unnecessary complications. Whether it's a personal or professional matter, follow your heart and trust that you know what's best for you.

Affirmation & Gratitude

"I trust my intuition, knowing that it guides me toward my highest good and truth."

Virgo
16 February 2025

Today Dear Virgo, it's a day to focus on self-care and personal well-being. You may have been pushing yourself hard recently, and today's energy encourages you to slow down and recharge. Take time to nourish your body, mind, and soul, whether through rest, relaxation, or indulging in something that brings you joy. Self-care is not a luxury—it's a necessity, and today is the perfect day to prioritize your health and happiness.

Affirmation & Gratitude

"I honor my need for self-care, knowing that by nourishing myself, I can give more to others."

Virgo
17 February 2025

Today Dear Virgo, your organizational skills are in high demand. You'll find satisfaction in creating order out of chaos, whether it's at work or home. Take the time to organize your space, schedule, or projects, and you'll feel a sense of accomplishment. Today's energy supports efficiency and structure, so don't hesitate to tackle any areas of your life that need tidying up. Your ability to bring order will lead to greater productivity and peace of mind.

Affirmation & Gratitude

"I create order and structure in my life, knowing that organization brings peace and clarity."

♍ Virgo
18 February 2025

Today Dear Virgo, your focus turns to personal growth and self-improvement. It's a great day to reflect on your goals and the steps you're taking to achieve them. If there's an area of your life that you've been wanting to improve, today's energy supports positive changes. Whether it's through learning, setting new intentions, or adopting healthy habits, today is a day for growth and progress. Trust that the changes you make today will lead to long-term success.

Affirmation & Gratitude

"I am committed to my personal growth and embrace positive changes that lead to a brighter future."

Virgo

19 February 2025

Today Dear Virgo, communication is key. Whether in your personal or professional life, your ability to express yourself clearly and thoughtfully will lead to positive results. Today's energy supports honest and open conversations, so don't be afraid to share your thoughts and feelings. You'll find that others are receptive to your words, and any misunderstandings can be resolved with ease. Be a good listener as well, as valuable insights can come from truly hearing others' perspectives.

Affirmation & Gratitude

"I communicate openly and honestly, trusting that clarity leads to stronger and healthier connections."

Virgo
20 February 2025

Today Dear Virgo, your analytical skills are heightened, making it a great day for problem-solving and critical thinking. Whether it's at work or in your personal life, you'll find satisfaction in breaking down complex issues and finding practical solutions. Don't hesitate to tackle any challenges that come your way—you have the skills and insight needed to navigate them successfully. Trust your ability to think clearly and strategically, and you'll achieve positive outcomes.

Affirmation & Gratitude

"I trust my analytical mind to find solutions and navigate challenges with clarity and focus."

 Virgo
21 February 2025

Today Dear Virgo, creativity is in the air. You may feel inspired to explore new ideas or express yourself through art, writing, or a personal project. Don't be afraid to think outside the box and try something different. Today's energy supports innovation and originality, so let your imagination run wild. Whether you're working on a creative endeavor or simply looking for fresh solutions to a problem, your unique perspective will lead to exciting breakthroughs.

Affirmation & Gratitude

"I embrace my creative spirit and allow it to inspire new ideas and possibilities in my life."

Virgo
22 February 2025

Today Dear Virgo, it's a great day to focus on relationships and connections with others. Whether it's spending quality time with loved ones, reaching out to friends, or building new connections, today's energy supports meaningful interactions. Be open to deepening your bonds and showing appreciation for the people in your life. Your kindness and warmth will be reciprocated, leading to stronger and more fulfilling relationships.

Affirmation & Gratitude

"I nurture my relationships with love and appreciation, knowing that meaningful connections bring joy and fulfillment."

Virgo
23 February 2025

Today Dear Virgo, your practical nature is in high demand. You'll find satisfaction in organizing and bringing structure to your day. Whether it's tidying up your workspace or streamlining your daily tasks, today's energy supports efficiency and productivity. Take the time to plan and prioritize, and you'll feel a sense of accomplishment by the end of the day. Don't hesitate to tackle any lingering tasks that require your attention. Your ability to focus and manage details will lead to success.

Affirmation & Gratitude

"I bring order and structure to my life, knowing that organization leads to peace and productivity."

Virgo
24 February 2025

Today Dear Virgo, it's a day for introspection and reflection. Take some quiet time to connect with your inner self and reflect on your personal journey. Journaling, meditation, or simply spending time in nature will help you gain clarity on your emotions and goals. This introspective time will provide valuable insights into your next steps. Don't rush through the day—allow yourself the space to sit with your thoughts and feelings. You'll emerge with a deeper understanding of yourself and your path forward.

Affirmation & Gratitude

"I honor moments of introspection, allowing myself the space to reflect and grow."

♍ Virgo
25 February 2025

Today Dear Virgo, your energy is focused on problem-solving. Whether at work or in your personal life, you'll have a clear vision of how to approach challenges. Use your analytical mind to break down complex issues into manageable steps, and you'll find solutions that benefit everyone involved. Today's energy supports practical thinking and attention to detail, so don't shy away from tackling tough tasks. Your efforts will lead to positive outcomes and progress.

Affirmation & Gratitude

"I trust my problem-solving abilities and approach challenges with clarity and focus."

Virgo

26 February 2025

Today Dear Virgo, self-care is a priority. You may feel the need to rest and recharge after a busy period. Take time to focus on your well-being, whether through physical rest, emotional nourishment, or simply slowing down. Listen to your body and honor its needs. Today's energy supports healing and renewal, so don't hesitate to take a break from the hustle and bustle. You'll return to your responsibilities feeling refreshed and ready to tackle what's ahead.

Affirmation & Gratitude

"I honor my body's need for rest and renewal, allowing myself to recharge and feel rejuvenated."

// Virgo
27 February 2025

Today Dear Virgo, communication is key. Whether in your personal or professional life, your ability to express yourself clearly and thoughtfully will lead to positive results. Today's energy supports honest and open conversations, so don't be afraid to share your thoughts and feelings. You'll find that others are receptive to your words, and any misunderstandings can be resolved with ease. Be a good listener as well, as valuable insights can come from truly hearing others' perspectives.

Affirmation & Gratitude

"I communicate with clarity and openness, trusting that honest conversations lead to understanding and connection."

Virgo
28 February 2025

Today Dear Virgo, it's a day for learning and expanding your knowledge. You may feel a strong desire to explore new subjects or dive deeper into a topic that interests you. Whether it's through reading, taking a course, or simply having intellectual conversations, today's energy supports growth and curiosity. Allow yourself to be a student of life, and you'll find joy in learning new things. The knowledge you gain today will serve you well in the future.

Affirmation & Gratitude

"I am grateful for my curiosity and the joy of learning and expanding my mind."

March 2025

 Virgo
01 March 2025

Today Dear Virgo, your energy is high, and you're ready to take on new challenges. Whether at work or in personal pursuits, your motivation will carry you far. Focus on tasks that require initiative and confidence, as today's energy supports bold actions. Your determination and drive will help you push through obstacles with ease. Trust in your abilities and don't hesitate to take the lead. Success is within reach, and your hard work will soon be rewarded.

Affirmation & Gratitude

"I am motivated and confident, ready to take bold actions toward my goals with clarity and focus."

Virgo
02 March 2025

Today Dear Virgo, relationships take center stage. Whether you're nurturing a romantic connection, deepening a friendship, or resolving conflicts, today's energy supports healing and growth in your relationships. Be open to heart-to-heart conversations and express your feelings with kindness. Others will appreciate your honesty and compassion, and your bonds will grow stronger as a result. This is a day to show love and appreciation for the important people in your life.

Affirmation & Gratitude

"I nurture my relationships with love, compassion, and understanding, knowing that strong connections bring joy and fulfillment."

Virgo

03 March 2025

Today Dear Virgo, you may feel the need for some alone time. It's a good day to retreat from the busyness of life and reconnect with yourself. Use this quiet time for introspection and self-reflection. Journaling or meditation will help you gain clarity on any unresolved issues or questions you've been grappling with. Don't rush through the day—take it slow and honor your need for solitude. You'll emerge with a clearer sense of direction and inner peace.

Affirmation & Gratitude

"I embrace moments of solitude, allowing myself time for introspection and clarity on my path forward."

Virgo
04 March 2025

Today Dear Virgo, your practical nature will shine through as you focus on organizing your day and managing your responsibilities. Today's energy supports productivity and attention to detail, making it a great day to tackle lingering tasks or projects that require precision. Take pride in your ability to bring order to chaos, and trust that your hard work will lead to positive results. By the end of the day, you'll feel a sense of accomplishment and satisfaction.

Affirmation & Gratitude

"I take pride in my ability to organize and manage details, knowing that my efforts lead to success and fulfillment."

Virgo
05 March 2025

Today Dear Virgo, you may feel a creative spark that inspires you to think outside the box. Whether it's through artistic expression or problem-solving, today's energy supports innovative ideas and fresh perspectives. Don't be afraid to explore new approaches to old challenges or to experiment with something different. Your creativity will lead to breakthroughs that open up new opportunities for growth and success. Let your imagination guide you toward new possibilities today.

Affirmation & Gratitude

"I embrace my creative spirit, allowing it to inspire new ideas and possibilities in my life."

 Virgo
06 March 2025

Today Dear Virgo, you'll find joy in connecting with others. Whether it's through work, friendships, or family, your social interactions will be positive and uplifting. Today's energy supports collaboration and teamwork, so don't hesitate to reach out for help or offer your support to others. Working together will lead to shared success and deepen your bonds with those around you. Trust in the power of community and the strength that comes from mutual support.

Affirmation & Gratitude

"I am grateful for the power of collaboration and the connections that bring joy and success into my life."

Virgo
07 March 2025

Today Dear Virgo, your focus turns to self-care and personal well-being. You may have been pushing yourself hard recently, and today's energy invites you to slow down and recharge. Take time to nourish your body, mind, and soul, whether through rest, relaxation, or indulging in something that brings you joy. Self-care is essential to maintaining balance and productivity, so don't hesitate to prioritize your health and happiness.

Affirmation & Gratitude

"I honor my need for self-care, knowing that by nurturing myself, I can give more to others and thrive."

Virgo
08 March 2025

Today Dear Virgo, it's a great day for learning and expanding your knowledge. Whether you're diving into a new subject, reading, or taking a course, today's energy supports intellectual growth. Allow yourself to be curious and explore topics that pique your interest. The knowledge you gain today will serve you well in the future and open up new opportunities for personal and professional growth. Embrace the joy of learning and trust that your curiosity will lead you in the right direction.

Affirmation & Gratitude

"I am grateful for my curiosity and the opportunities for learning that help me grow and evolve."

Virgo

09 March 2025

Today Dear Virgo, balance is the theme. It's important to find harmony between your responsibilities and your personal well-being. You may have been juggling multiple tasks, but today's energy invites you to slow down and create balance in your life. Focus on your priorities and let go of anything that's no longer serving you. By finding equilibrium, you'll feel more centered and less overwhelmed. Take time for self-care and relaxation to restore your energy.

Affirmation & Gratitude

"I create balance in my life, knowing that harmony between work and rest leads to peace and fulfillment."

Virgo
10 March 2025

Today Dear Virgo, it's a day for closure. Whether it's completing a project, resolving an issue, or letting go of something that's been holding you back, today's energy supports finishing what you've started. By tying up loose ends, you'll create space for new opportunities and experiences. Don't be afraid to close one chapter to open another—you're making room for growth and success.

Affirmation & Gratitude

"I embrace the power of closure, knowing that completing tasks creates space for new beginnings and opportunities."

 Virgo
11 March 2025

Today Dear Virgo, teamwork is key. Whether you're collaborating with colleagues, friends, or family, today's energy supports working together toward a common goal. Your ability to contribute your strengths to the group will lead to greater success than you could achieve on your own. Don't hesitate to share your ideas and offer support to others. Together, you'll accomplish more than you ever imagined. Trust in the power of collaboration.

Affirmation & Gratitude

"I am grateful for the power of teamwork, knowing that together we can achieve more than we can alone."

 Virgo
12 March 2025

Today Dear Virgo, you'll feel a burst of motivation and energy. It's a great day to start something new or make significant progress on a project you've been working on. Your enthusiasm and determination will help you overcome obstacles and move forward with confidence. Use this energy to take bold actions and pursue your goals. Success is within reach, so stay focused and committed to your vision.

Affirmation & Gratitude

"I am motivated and determined, ready to take bold steps toward my goals with confidence and clarity."

 Virgo
13 March 2025

Today Dear Virgo, your attention to detail will be an asset as you focus on tasks that require precision and thoroughness. Whether it's at work or in your personal life, your meticulous nature will help you accomplish tasks with accuracy and success. Take your time to ensure that everything is done correctly, and don't rush through anything. By paying attention to the finer details, you'll achieve the results you desire.

Affirmation & Gratitude

"I take pride in my attention to detail, knowing that it leads to success and satisfaction in all I do."

Virgo

14 March 2025

Today Dear Virgo, love and relationships are highlighted. Whether you're deepening a romantic connection, spending time with family, or reconnecting with friends, today's energy supports nurturing your bonds. Show appreciation for the people you care about and express your feelings openly. Your warmth and affection will be reciprocated, leading to stronger and more meaningful relationships. Trust in the power of love and connection to bring joy into your life.

Affirmation & Gratitude

"I nurture love and connection in my life, knowing that strong relationships bring joy and fulfillment."

 Virgo
15 March 2025

Today Dear Virgo, your intuition is heightened, and you may find that your gut feelings are guiding you in the right direction. Trust your instincts, especially when making decisions. Your inner wisdom is strong, and by listening to it, you'll avoid unnecessary complications. Whether it's a personal or professional matter, follow your heart and trust that you know what's best for you.

Affirmation & Gratitude

"I trust my intuition, knowing that it guides me toward my highest good and truth."

 Virgo
16 March 2025

Today Dear Virgo, your energy is focused on personal well-being. Take time to recharge and focus on self-care, whether through physical rest, emotional nourishment, or simply slowing down. Today's energy supports healing and renewal, so don't hesitate to take a break from the hustle and bustle. You'll return to your responsibilities feeling refreshed and ready to tackle what's ahead with a clear mind and a renewed sense of purpose.

Affirmation & Gratitude

"I honor my need for self-care, knowing that by nourishing myself, I can give more to others and thrive."

 Virgo
17 March 2025

Today Dear Virgo, your organizational skills are in high demand. You'll find satisfaction in bringing order to chaos, whether at work or home. Take the time to organize your space, schedule, or projects, and you'll feel a sense of accomplishment. Today's energy supports efficiency and structure, so don't hesitate to tackle any areas of your life that need tidying up. Your ability to bring order will lead to greater productivity and peace of mind.

Affirmation & Gratitude

"I create order and structure in my life, knowing that organization brings peace and clarity."

Virgo

18 March 2025

Today Dear Virgo, your focus turns to personal growth and self-improvement. It's a great day to reflect on your goals and the steps you're taking to achieve them. If there's an area of your life that you've been wanting to improve, today's energy supports positive changes. Whether it's through learning, setting new intentions, or adopting healthy habits, today is a day for growth and progress. Trust that the changes you make today will lead to long-term success.

Affirmation & Gratitude

"I am committed to my personal growth and embrace positive changes that lead to a brighter future."

Virgo

19 March 2025

Today Dear Virgo, communication is key. Whether in your personal or professional life, your ability to express yourself clearly and thoughtfully will lead to positive results. Today's energy supports honest and open conversations, so don't be afraid to share your thoughts and feelings. You'll find that others are receptive to your words, and any misunderstandings can be resolved with ease. Be a good listener as well, as valuable insights can come from truly hearing others' perspectives.

Affirmation & Gratitude

"I communicate openly and honestly, trusting that clarity leads to stronger and healthier connections."

Virgo

20 March 2025

Today Dear Virgo, your analytical skills are heightened, making it a great day for problem-solving and critical thinking. Whether it's at work or in your personal life, you'll find satisfaction in breaking down complex issues and finding practical solutions. Don't hesitate to tackle any challenges that come your way—you have the skills and insight needed to navigate them successfully. Trust your ability to think clearly and strategically, and you'll achieve positive outcomes.

Affirmation & Gratitude

"I trust my analytical mind to find solutions and navigate challenges with clarity and focus."

 Virgo
21 March 2025

Today Dear Virgo, creativity is in the air. You may feel inspired to explore new ideas or express yourself through art, writing, or a personal project. Don't be afraid to think outside the box and try something different. Today's energy supports innovation and originality, so let your imagination run wild. Whether you're working on a creative endeavor or simply looking for fresh solutions to a problem, your unique perspective will lead to exciting breakthroughs.

Affirmation & Gratitude

"I embrace my creative spirit and allow it to inspire new ideas and possibilities in my life."

Virgo
22 March 2025

Today Dear Virgo, it's a great day to focus on relationships and connections with others. Whether it's spending quality time with loved ones, reaching out to friends, or building new connections, today's energy supports meaningful interactions. Be open to deepening your bonds and showing appreciation for the people in your life. Your kindness and warmth will be reciprocated, leading to stronger and more fulfilling relationships.

Affirmation & Gratitude

"I nurture my relationships with love and appreciation, knowing that meaningful connections bring joy and fulfillment."

Virgo

23 March 2025

Today Dear Virgo, your practical nature is in high demand. You'll find satisfaction in organizing and bringing structure to your day. Whether it's tidying up your workspace or streamlining your daily tasks, today's energy supports efficiency and productivity. Take the time to plan and prioritize, and you'll feel a sense of accomplishment by the end of the day. Don't hesitate to tackle any lingering tasks that require your attention. Your ability to focus and manage details will lead to success.

Affirmation & Gratitude

"I bring order and structure to my life, knowing that organization leads to peace and productivity."

Virgo
24 March 2025

Today Dear Virgo, it's a day for introspection and reflection. Take some quiet time to connect with your inner self and reflect on your personal journey. Journaling, meditation, or simply spending time in nature will help you gain clarity on your emotions and goals. This introspective time will provide valuable insights into your next steps. Don't rush through the day—allow yourself the space to sit with your thoughts and feelings. You'll emerge with a deeper understanding of yourself and your path forward.

Affirmation & Gratitude

"I honor moments of introspection, allowing myself the space to reflect and grow."

 Virgo
25 March 2025

Today Dear Virgo, your energy is focused on problem-solving. Whether at work or in your personal life, you'll have a clear vision of how to approach challenges. Use your analytical mind to break down complex issues into manageable steps, and you'll find solutions that benefit everyone involved. Today's energy supports practical thinking and attention to detail, so don't shy away from tackling tough tasks. Your efforts will lead to positive outcomes and progress.

Affirmation & Gratitude

"I trust my problem-solving abilities and approach challenges with clarity and focus."

Virgo
26 March 2025

Today Dear Virgo, self-care is a priority. You may feel the need to rest and recharge after a busy period. Take time to focus on your well-being, whether through physical rest, emotional nourishment, or simply slowing down. Listen to your body and honor its needs. Today's energy supports healing and renewal, so don't hesitate to take a break from the hustle and bustle. You'll return to your responsibilities feeling refreshed and ready to tackle what's ahead.

Affirmation & Gratitude

"I honor my body's need for rest and renewal, allowing myself to recharge and feel rejuvenated."

Virgo
27 March 2025

Today Dear Virgo, communication is key. Whether in your personal or professional life, your ability to express yourself clearly and thoughtfully will lead to positive results. Today's energy supports honest and open conversations, so don't be afraid to share your thoughts and feelings. You'll find that others are receptive to your words, and any misunderstandings can be resolved with ease. Be a good listener as well, as valuable insights can come from truly hearing others' perspectives.

Affirmation & Gratitude

"I communicate with clarity and openness, trusting that honest conversations lead to understanding and connection."

Virgo
28 March 2025

Today Dear Virgo, it's a day for learning and expanding your knowledge. You may feel a strong desire to explore new subjects or dive deeper into a topic that interests you. Whether it's through reading, taking a course, or simply having intellectual conversations, today's energy supports growth and curiosity. Allow yourself to be a student of life, and you'll find joy in learning new things. The knowledge you gain today will serve you well in the future.

Affirmation & Gratitude

"I am grateful for my curiosity and the joy of learning and expanding my mind."

 Virgo
29 March 2025

Today Dear Virgo, your creativity is flowing. Whether you're working on a personal project, solving a problem, or finding new ways to approach a challenge, today's energy supports thinking outside the box. Don't be afraid to experiment with new ideas or take a different approach. Your innovative thinking will lead to exciting breakthroughs and positive results. Trust in your creative abilities and let them guide you toward new solutions.

Affirmation & Gratitude

"I embrace my creative spirit, allowing it to lead me toward new ideas and exciting possibilities."

 Virgo
30 March 2025

Today Dear Virgo, your focus turns to relationships. Whether romantic, familial, or friendships, today is a day to nurture your connections and show appreciation for the people in your life. Reach out to someone you haven't spoken to in a while, or simply spend quality time with loved ones. Your kindness and warmth will strengthen your bonds and bring joy to those around you. By prioritizing your relationships today, you'll create deeper and more meaningful connections.

Affirmation & Gratitude

"I am grateful for the love and support of those around me, and I nurture my relationships with care and kindness."

 Virgo
31 March 2025

Today Dear Virgo, balance is essential. You may have been juggling multiple responsibilities, but today's energy invites you to create harmony between work and rest. Take time to evaluate your priorities and ensure that you're giving equal attention to your personal well-being. By finding balance, you'll feel more centered and ready to tackle your tasks with clarity and focus. Prioritize self-care and relaxation to maintain your overall sense of well-being.

Affirmation & Gratitude

"I create balance in my life, knowing that harmony between work and rest leads to peace and fulfillment."

April 2025

Virgo
01 April 2025

Today Dear Virgo, the energy supports a fresh start. Whether you're beginning a new project or setting new goals, today's energy encourages you to take the first step with confidence. Don't be afraid to explore new possibilities and embrace change. Your practical nature will guide you in making smart, informed decisions. Trust that new beginnings are leading you toward personal and professional growth. Be open to the opportunities that come your way today.

Affirmation & Gratitude

"I embrace new beginnings with confidence, trusting that each step leads me toward growth and success."

Virgo
02 April 2025

Today Dear Virgo, your attention to detail will be a valuable asset. Whether at work or home, today's energy supports organization and precision. Focus on completing tasks that require careful attention, and take your time to ensure everything is done correctly. Your meticulous nature will help you achieve high-quality results, and others will appreciate your thoroughness. Don't rush through anything today—allow yourself the time to produce the best possible outcome.

Affirmation & Gratitude

"I take pride in my attention to detail, knowing that it leads to excellence and success in all I do."

 Virgo
03 April 2025

Today Dear Virgo, you may feel a pull toward introspection. It's a good day to step back from the busyness of life and spend time reflecting on your personal goals and emotions. Quiet time alone will provide clarity and insight into your next steps. Journaling, meditation, or simply spending time in nature will help you connect with your inner self. Trust the wisdom that comes from stillness, and allow it to guide your future decisions.

Affirmation & Gratitude

"I honor moments of quiet reflection, trusting that introspection leads to clarity and personal growth."

Virgo
04 April 2025

Today Dear Virgo, relationships are highlighted. You'll find joy in connecting with others, whether through deep conversations or acts of kindness. Today's energy supports open-hearted communication, so don't hesitate to express your feelings. Nurturing your bonds with loved ones will strengthen your relationships and bring greater understanding and harmony. Be a good listener and offer your support to those who need it. Your compassion and kindness will be appreciated.

Affirmation & Gratitude

"I nurture my relationships with love and understanding, knowing that strong connections bring joy and fulfillment."

 # Virgo
05 April 2025

Today Dear Virgo, creativity flows easily, and you may feel inspired to try something new. Whether you're working on an artistic project, problem-solving, or exploring a new hobby, today's energy supports innovation. Don't be afraid to think outside the box and take risks. Your unique perspective will lead to exciting breakthroughs and open doors to new possibilities. Let your imagination guide you and enjoy the process of creative exploration.

Affirmation & Gratitude

"I embrace my creativity, allowing it to lead me toward new ideas and exciting possibilities in my life."

Virgo
06 April 2025

Today Dear Virgo, balance is key. You may be juggling multiple responsibilities, but it's important to find harmony between work and relaxation. Take time to prioritize your tasks and focus on what's most important. Don't overextend yourself—remember to make room for self-care and relaxation. By creating balance, you'll feel more centered and capable of handling everything on your plate. Trust that balance leads to peace and productivity.

Affirmation & Gratitude

"I create balance in my life, knowing that harmony between work and rest leads to inner peace and fulfillment."

Virgo
07 April 2025

Today Dear Virgo, teamwork is emphasized. Whether you're collaborating on a work project or spending time with friends or family, today's energy supports cooperation and shared success. Don't hesitate to lean on others for support, and be open to contributing your strengths to the group. Working together will lead to greater achievements than going it alone. Trust in the power of collaboration and the value of community.

Affirmation & Gratitude

"I am grateful for the power of teamwork, knowing that collaboration leads to shared success and deeper connections."

Virgo
08 April 2025

Today Dear Virgo, self-care is essential. You've been working hard, and today's energy encourages you to slow down and focus on your well-being. Take time to rest and recharge, whether through physical relaxation, emotional nourishment, or simply taking a break from your responsibilities. By prioritizing self-care, you'll restore your energy and return to your tasks with renewed vitality. Don't underestimate the power of rest—it's a necessary part of maintaining balance and productivity.

Affirmation & Gratitude

"I honor my body's need for rest and renewal, allowing myself time to recharge and feel rejuvenated."

# Virgo
09 April 2025

Today Dear Virgo, your practical nature is in high demand. Whether you're managing a project, organizing your space, or planning for the future, today's energy supports logical thinking and attention to detail. Take the time to approach tasks methodically and ensure that everything is in order. Your ability to plan and organize will lead to success and a sense of accomplishment. Trust in your practical skills to navigate challenges and achieve your goals.

Affirmation & Gratitude

"I trust in my practical nature and attention to detail to guide me toward success and accomplishment."

Virgo
10 April 2025

Today Dear Virgo, you may feel a burst of creative energy. Whether you're working on a personal project, solving a problem, or finding new ways to approach a challenge, today's energy supports thinking outside the box. Don't be afraid to experiment with new ideas or take a different approach. Your innovative thinking will lead to exciting breakthroughs and positive results. Trust in your creative abilities and let them guide you toward new solutions.

Affirmation & Gratitude

"I embrace my creative spirit, allowing it to lead me toward new ideas and exciting possibilities."

Virgo
11 April 2025

Today Dear Virgo, relationships take center stage. Whether you're spending time with family, friends, or a romantic partner, today is a day to nurture your connections. Show appreciation for the people who matter most to you, and make an effort to strengthen your bonds. Meaningful conversations and acts of kindness will go a long way in deepening your relationships. Be present and open-hearted, and you'll find that your connections grow stronger.

Affirmation & Gratitude

"I nurture my relationships with love and care, knowing that strong connections bring joy and fulfillment."

Virgo
12 April 2025

Today Dear Virgo, your analytical mind is sharp, making it a great day for problem-solving and tackling complex tasks. Whether it's at work or in your personal life, you'll find satisfaction in breaking down challenges and finding practical solutions. Take your time to think things through and approach each task with logic and precision. Your efforts will lead to successful outcomes and a sense of accomplishment. Trust in your ability to navigate any challenges that come your way.

Affirmation & Gratitude

"I trust my analytical mind to find solutions and navigate challenges with clarity and focus."

 Virgo
13 April 2025

Today Dear Virgo, it's a great day for self-reflection and personal growth. Take some time to think about your goals, values, and the direction you want to take in life. Today's energy supports introspection and planning for the future. Use this time to gain clarity on what matters most to you and make a plan for moving forward. Trust in your inner wisdom to guide your decisions and help you create a fulfilling path.

Affirmation & Gratitude

"I embrace moments of self-reflection, trusting that clarity and personal growth come from within."

Virgo
14 April 2025

Today Dear Virgo, creativity is flowing, and today's energy supports thinking outside the box. Whether you're working on a creative project or looking for fresh solutions to a problem, your imagination will lead you to exciting new possibilities. Don't be afraid to experiment with different approaches or explore new ideas. Your unique perspective will help you discover breakthroughs that others might overlook. Let your creativity shine today and trust in your innovative spirit.

Affirmation & Gratitude

"I embrace my creativity, allowing it to guide me toward new ideas and exciting opportunities."

Virgo
15 April 2025

Today Dear Virgo, communication is key. Whether you're resolving conflicts, having important conversations, or simply connecting with others, your ability to express yourself clearly and thoughtfully will lead to positive outcomes. Be open and honest in your communication, and make an effort to listen to others with empathy. By fostering clear and respectful dialogue, you'll strengthen your relationships and build trust. Don't hesitate to address any misunderstandings—today is a day for healing through communication.

Affirmation & Gratitude

"I communicate openly and honestly, trusting that clarity and understanding lead to stronger connections."

Virgo
16 April 2025

Today Dear Virgo, self-care takes priority. You may have been feeling drained, and today's energy encourages you to slow down and focus on your well-being. Whether through physical rest, emotional self-care, or simply taking a break, allow yourself time to recharge. By nurturing yourself, you'll restore your energy and regain a sense of balance. Don't feel guilty about taking time for yourself—it's an essential part of staying healthy and productive.

Affirmation & Gratitude

"I honor my body's need for rest and rejuvenation, knowing that self-care is essential for my well-being."

 Virgo
17 April 2025

Today Dear Virgo, balance is essential. You may be juggling multiple responsibilities, but it's important to find harmony between work and personal life. Today's energy supports creating structure and prioritizing your tasks. Focus on what's most important and don't hesitate to delegate or let go of anything that's no longer serving you. By achieving balance, you'll feel more centered and able to handle your day with ease. Trust that balance leads to peace and fulfillment.

Affirmation & Gratitude

"I create balance in my life, knowing that harmony between work and rest brings peace and fulfillment."

Virgo
18 April 2025

Today Dear Virgo, it's a day for collaboration. Whether you're working on a team project, brainstorming with colleagues, or spending time with friends, today's energy supports cooperation and shared success. Be open to other people's ideas and contributions, and don't hesitate to offer your own insights. Working together will lead to greater achievements than you could accomplish alone. Trust in the power of teamwork and the value of community.

Affirmation & Gratitude

"I am grateful for the power of collaboration, knowing that shared efforts lead to greater success and stronger connections."

 Virgo
19 April 2025

Today Dear Virgo, your practical side will shine as you focus on organizing and planning for the future. Whether it's at work or in your personal life, today's energy supports logical thinking and careful attention to detail. Take the time to create a clear plan for your goals, and don't rush through anything. Your ability to organize and plan will set you up for success. Trust in your practical nature to guide you in making smart decisions.

Affirmation & Gratitude

"I trust my practical nature and attention to detail to guide me toward success and fulfillment."

Virgo
20 April 2025

Today Dear Virgo, your creativity is in full bloom. Whether you're working on a personal project, solving a problem, or exploring a new idea, today's energy supports thinking outside the box. Don't be afraid to experiment with different approaches or explore new possibilities. Your imagination will lead you to exciting breakthroughs and new opportunities. Trust in your creative spirit and let it guide you toward success.

Affirmation & Gratitude

"I embrace my creative spirit, allowing it to lead me toward new ideas and exciting opportunities."

 Virgo
21 April 2025

Today Dear Virgo, your focus turns to relationships. Whether it's deepening a romantic connection, spending time with family, or nurturing friendships, today's energy supports strengthening your bonds with others. Make an effort to show appreciation for the people who matter most to you, and don't hesitate to reach out and express your feelings. Meaningful conversations and acts of kindness will go a long way in deepening your connections.

Affirmation & Gratitude

"I nurture my relationships with love and care, knowing that strong connections bring joy and fulfillment."

Virgo
22 April 2025

Today Dear Virgo, it's a great day for personal growth and self-improvement. Take some time to reflect on your goals and values, and think about the changes you'd like to make in your life. Whether it's learning something new, setting new intentions, or adopting healthier habits, today's energy supports positive change. Trust in your ability to grow and evolve, and take the first step toward becoming the best version of yourself.

Affirmation & Gratitude

"I embrace personal growth and trust in my ability to make positive changes that lead to a fulfilling life."

Virgo

23 April 2025

Today Dear Virgo, communication is key. Whether you're resolving conflicts, having important conversations, or simply connecting with others, your ability to express yourself clearly and thoughtfully will lead to positive outcomes. Be open and honest in your communication, and make an effort to listen to others with empathy. By fostering clear and respectful dialogue, you'll strengthen your relationships and build trust. Don't hesitate to address any misunderstandings—today is a day for healing through communication.

Affirmation & Gratitude

"I communicate openly and honestly, trusting that clarity and understanding lead to stronger connections."

Virgo
24 April 2025

Today Dear Virgo, you may feel the need for introspection. It's a good day to step back from the busyness of life and spend time reflecting on your personal goals and emotions. Quiet time alone will provide clarity and insight into your next steps. Journaling, meditation, or simply spending time in nature will help you connect with your inner self. Trust the wisdom that comes from stillness, and allow it to guide your future decisions.

Affirmation & Gratitude

"I honor moments of quiet reflection, trusting that introspection leads to clarity and personal growth."

 Virgo
25 April 2025

Today Dear Virgo, your focus is on productivity and getting things done. Whether it's tackling a project at work or handling tasks at home, today's energy supports efficiency and attention to detail. Take advantage of this boost in motivation to complete lingering tasks and organize your day for maximum productivity. Your practical nature will guide you in prioritizing what needs to be done, and you'll feel a sense of accomplishment by the day's end.

Affirmation & Gratitude

"I am focused and productive, trusting that my efforts today lead to success and fulfillment."

 Virgo
26 April 2025

Today Dear Virgo, it's a great day for learning and expanding your knowledge. Whether you're diving into a new subject, reading, or taking a course, today's energy supports intellectual growth. Allow yourself to be curious and explore topics that pique your interest. The knowledge you gain today will serve you well in the future and open up new opportunities for personal and professional growth. Embrace the joy of learning and trust that your curiosity will lead you in the right direction.

Affirmation & Gratitude

"I am grateful for my curiosity and the opportunities for learning that help me grow and evolve."

Virgo
27 April 2025

Today Dear Virgo, balance is key. You may be juggling multiple responsibilities, but it's important to find harmony between work and relaxation. Take time to prioritize your tasks and focus on what's most important. Don't overextend yourself—remember to make room for self-care and relaxation. By creating balance, you'll feel more centered and capable of handling everything on your plate. Trust that balance leads to peace and productivity.

Affirmation & Gratitude

"I create balance in my life, knowing that harmony between work and rest leads to inner peace and fulfillment."

Virgo
28 April 2025

Today Dear Virgo, teamwork is emphasized. Whether you're collaborating on a work project or spending time with friends or family, today's energy supports cooperation and shared success. Don't hesitate to lean on others for support, and be open to contributing your strengths to the group. Working together will lead to greater achievements than going it alone. Trust in the power of collaboration and the value of community.

Affirmation & Gratitude

"I am grateful for the power of teamwork, knowing that collaboration leads to shared success and deeper connections."

 Virgo
29 April 2025

Today Dear Virgo, self-care is essential. You've been working hard, and today's energy encourages you to slow down and focus on your well-being. Take time to rest and recharge, whether through physical relaxation, emotional nourishment, or simply taking a break from your responsibilities. By prioritizing self-care, you'll restore your energy and return to your tasks with renewed vitality. Don't underestimate the power of rest—it's a necessary part of maintaining balance and productivity.

Affirmation & Gratitude

"I honor my body's need for rest and renewal, allowing myself time to recharge and feel rejuvenated."

Virgo

30 April 2025

Today Dear Virgo, it's a great day for learning and expanding your knowledge. Whether you're diving into a new subject, reading, or taking a course, today's energy supports intellectual growth. Allow yourself to be curious and explore topics that pique your interest. The knowledge you gain today will serve you well in the future and open up new opportunities for personal and professional growth. Embrace the joy of learning and trust that your curiosity will lead you in the right direction.

Affirmation & Gratitude

"I am grateful for my curiosity and the opportunities for learning that help me grow and evolve."

May 2025

Virgo

01 May 2025

Today Dear Virgo, the energy supports new beginnings and fresh perspectives. Whether you're starting a new project or embracing a new mindset, today's energy invites you to approach everything with an open heart. Let go of any fear or doubt, and step confidently into this new phase. Trust in your ability to make the best of new opportunities, and stay focused on your long-term vision. Today is a great day for setting intentions and planting seeds for future success.

Affirmation & Gratitude

"I embrace new beginnings with confidence, trusting that every step forward leads to growth and success."

Virgo

02 May 2025

Today Dear Virgo, your analytical nature is your greatest asset. Whether you're tackling complex tasks or organizing your day, your ability to see the details will help you succeed. Today's energy supports problem-solving and practical thinking, so don't hesitate to dive deep into tasks that require precision. Your efforts will pay off, and you'll feel a sense of accomplishment by the end of the day. Take pride in your ability to handle challenges with clarity and focus.

Affirmation & Gratitude

"I trust my analytical mind to navigate challenges and approach tasks with clarity and precision."

Virgo
03 May 2025

Today Dear Virgo, it's a great day to focus on personal growth and reflection. Take time to evaluate where you are in your journey and where you want to go next. Journaling, meditation, or quiet reflection will help you gain insight into your next steps. This is a time for planning and envisioning the future. Don't rush the process—allow yourself space to think deeply about your goals and values.

Affirmation & Gratitude

"I trust my inner wisdom to guide me toward clarity and personal growth."

Virgo
04 May 2025

Today Dear Virgo, relationships take center stage. Whether with friends, family, or romantic partners, today is a good day to nurture your connections. Reach out to someone you care about, offer a helping hand, or simply spend quality time together. Strengthening your bonds will bring joy and fulfillment. Open your heart to love and understanding, and you'll find that your relationships deepen and grow stronger.

Affirmation & Gratitude

"I nurture my relationships with love and care, knowing that strong connections bring joy and fulfillment."

Virgo
05 May 2025

Today Dear Virgo, balance is essential. You may be juggling multiple responsibilities, but it's important to find harmony between work and relaxation. Take time to prioritize your tasks and focus on what's most important. Don't overextend yourself—remember to make room for self-care and relaxation. By creating balance, you'll feel more centered and capable of handling everything on your plate. Trust that balance leads to peace and productivity.

Affirmation & Gratitude

"I create balance in my life, knowing that harmony between work and rest leads to inner peace and fulfillment."

Virgo
06 May 2025

Today Dear Virgo, your practical nature will shine as you focus on organizing and planning for the future. Whether it's at work or in your personal life, today's energy supports logical thinking and careful attention to detail. Take the time to create a clear plan for your goals, and don't rush through anything. Your ability to organize and plan will set you up for success. Trust in your practical nature to guide you in making smart decisions.

Affirmation & Gratitude

"I trust my practical nature and attention to detail to guide me toward success and fulfillment."

 Virgo
07 May 2025

Today Dear Virgo, creativity is flowing. Whether you're working on a personal project, solving a problem, or exploring a new idea, today's energy supports thinking outside the box. Don't be afraid to experiment with different approaches or explore new possibilities. Your imagination will lead you to exciting breakthroughs and new opportunities. Trust in your creative spirit and let it guide you toward success.

Affirmation & Gratitude

"I embrace my creative spirit, allowing it to lead me toward new ideas and exciting opportunities."

Virgo
08 May 2025

Today Dear Virgo, teamwork is emphasized. Whether you're collaborating on a project or spending time with friends and family, today's energy supports cooperation and shared success. Be open to other people's ideas and contributions, and don't hesitate to offer your own insights. Working together will lead to greater achievements than you could accomplish alone. Trust in the power of collaboration and the value of community.

Affirmation & Gratitude

"I am grateful for the power of teamwork, knowing that collaboration leads to shared success and deeper connections."

 Virgo
09 May 2025

Today Dear Virgo, your focus turns inward, and it's a good day for introspection. Spend some time reflecting on your goals and values, and think about where you're headed in life. Journaling, meditation, or simply quiet reflection will help you gain clarity and insight. This is a time for deep thinking and self-awareness, so don't rush through the process. Allow yourself the space to consider your next steps with care and intention.

Affirmation & Gratitude

"I trust my inner voice to guide me toward clarity and self-awareness."

Virgo

10 May 2025

Today Dear Virgo, communication is key. Whether at work or in your personal life, your ability to express yourself clearly and thoughtfully will lead to positive outcomes. Today's energy supports honest conversations and resolution of any misunderstandings. Be open to hearing others' perspectives, and approach conversations with empathy. By fostering clear and respectful dialogue, you'll strengthen your relationships and build trust.

Affirmation & Gratitude

"I communicate openly and honestly, trusting that clarity and understanding lead to stronger connections."

 # Virgo
11 May 2025

Today Dear Virgo, your attention to detail will be your greatest strength. Whether you're organizing your space, completing a project, or planning for the future, your ability to see the finer points will lead to success. Today's energy supports meticulous work and careful planning, so don't rush through anything. Take the time to do things right, and you'll feel a sense of accomplishment by the end of the day.

Affirmation & Gratitude

"I take pride in my attention to detail, knowing that it leads to excellence and success."

 Virgo
12 May 2025

Today Dear Virgo, your focus turns to relationships. Today is a good day to strengthen your bonds with loved ones, whether through quality time, meaningful conversations, or acts of kindness. Be present and attentive to the needs of those around you, and you'll find that your connections deepen and grow stronger. Love and understanding will flow easily today, bringing joy to your relationships.

Affirmation & Gratitude

"I nurture my relationships with love and care, knowing that strong connections bring joy and fulfillment."

 Virgo
13 May 2025

Today Dear Virgo, self-care is essential. You may have been pushing yourself hard lately, and today's energy encourages you to slow down and recharge. Whether it's physical rest, emotional nourishment, or simply taking a break from responsibilities, prioritize your well-being today. By taking care of yourself, you'll restore your energy and be better equipped to handle future challenges. Don't feel guilty for resting—self-care is a vital part of maintaining balance and health.

Affirmation & Gratitude

"I honor my body's need for rest and renewal, knowing that self-care is essential for my well-being."

Virgo

14 May 2025

Today Dear Virgo, creativity is in the air. Whether you're working on a personal project, solving a problem, or exploring new ideas, today's energy supports thinking outside the box. Don't be afraid to experiment with new approaches or try something different. Your unique perspective will lead to exciting breakthroughs and fresh opportunities. Trust in your creative abilities and let your imagination guide you toward success.

Affirmation & Gratitude

"I embrace my creative spirit, allowing it to guide me toward new ideas and exciting opportunities."

Virgo

15 May 2025

Today Dear Virgo, balance is key. You may feel pulled in different directions, but it's important to create harmony between your work and personal life. Prioritize your tasks and make room for relaxation and self-care. By maintaining balance, you'll feel more grounded and able to handle your responsibilities with ease. Trust that finding equilibrium will lead to greater peace and productivity.

Affirmation & Gratitude

"I create balance in my life, knowing that harmony between work and rest leads to peace and fulfillment."

Virgo

16 May 2025

Today Dear Virgo, your practical nature is in high demand. Whether you're managing a project, organizing your home, or planning for the future, today's energy supports logical thinking and careful attention to detail. Take the time to approach tasks methodically and ensure that everything is in order. Your ability to plan and organize will lead to success and a sense of accomplishment. Trust in your practical skills to navigate challenges and achieve your goals.

Affirmation & Gratitude

"I trust in my practical nature and attention to detail to guide me toward success and accomplishment."

Virgo
17 May 2025

Today Dear Virgo, relationships are highlighted. Whether you're spending time with family, friends, or a romantic partner, today is a day to nurture your connections. Show appreciation for the people who matter most to you, and make an effort to strengthen your bonds. Meaningful conversations and acts of kindness will go a long way in deepening your relationships. Be present and open-hearted, and you'll find that your connections grow stronger.

Affirmation & Gratitude

"I nurture my relationships with love and care, knowing that strong connections bring joy and fulfillment."

Virgo

18 May 2025

Today Dear Virgo, you may feel the need for introspection and reflection. It's a good day to take a step back from the busyness of life and spend time thinking about your personal goals and emotions. Quiet time alone will provide clarity and insight into your next steps. Trust the wisdom that comes from within, and allow it to guide your decisions. By tuning into your inner voice, you'll gain the clarity you need to move forward confidently.

Affirmation & Gratitude

"I honor moments of introspection, trusting that inner wisdom leads to clarity and self-awareness."

Virgo
19 May 2025

Today Dear Virgo, teamwork is emphasized. Whether you're working on a project with colleagues or collaborating with loved ones, today's energy supports cooperation and shared success. Be open to other people's ideas and contributions, and don't hesitate to offer your own insights. Working together will lead to greater achievements than you could accomplish alone. Trust in the power of teamwork and the value of community.

Affirmation & Gratitude

"I am grateful for the power of teamwork, knowing that collaboration leads to shared success and deeper connections."

Virgo

20 May 2025

Today Dear Virgo, self-care is a priority. You've been busy lately, and today's energy encourages you to slow down and focus on your well-being. Whether through rest, relaxation, or emotional nourishment, take time to recharge. By taking care of yourself, you'll restore your energy and feel more balanced. Don't underestimate the power of rest—it's an important part of maintaining health and productivity.

Affirmation & Gratitude

"I honor my body's need for rest and renewal, knowing that self-care is essential for my well-being."

Virgo

21 May 2025

Today Dear Virgo, communication is key. Whether you're resolving a conflict, having an important conversation, or simply connecting with others, your ability to express yourself clearly and thoughtfully will lead to positive outcomes. Be open to listening to others and offering your perspective with kindness. By fostering clear and respectful dialogue, you'll strengthen your relationships and build trust. Don't hesitate to address any misunderstandings—today is a day for healing through communication.

Affirmation & Gratitude

"I communicate openly and honestly, trusting that clarity and understanding lead to stronger connections."

Virgo

22 May 2025

Today Dear Virgo, your practical side will be an asset as you focus on organizing your day and managing your responsibilities. Today's energy supports productivity and attention to detail, making it a great day to tackle tasks that require focus. Don't rush through anything—take your time to ensure that everything is done correctly. Your practical approach will lead to success and a sense of accomplishment. By the end of the day, you'll feel satisfied with your efforts.

Affirmation & Gratitude

"I trust in my practical nature to guide me toward success and fulfillment in all that I do."

 Virgo
23 May 2025

Today Dear Virgo, balance is key. You may feel pulled in different directions, but it's important to create harmony between your work and personal life. Prioritize your tasks and make room for relaxation and self-care. By maintaining balance, you'll feel more grounded and able to handle your responsibilities with ease. Trust that finding equilibrium will lead to greater peace and productivity.

Affirmation & Gratitude

"I create balance in my life, knowing that harmony between work and rest leads to peace and fulfillment."

Virgo

24 May 2025

Today Dear Virgo, your creative spirit is alive. Whether you're working on a project, solving a problem, or thinking about a new idea, today's energy supports creativity and innovation. Don't be afraid to think outside the box and try something new. Your unique perspective will lead to breakthroughs and fresh opportunities. Trust in your creative abilities and let your imagination guide you toward success.

Affirmation & Gratitude

"I embrace my creative spirit, allowing it to guide me toward new ideas and exciting opportunities."

Virgo
25 May 2025

Today Dear Virgo, relationships take center stage. It's a good day to strengthen your bonds with loved ones and express your appreciation for the people who matter most. Whether through quality time, thoughtful gestures, or open conversations, your efforts will deepen your connections and bring joy to your relationships. Be present and attentive, and you'll find that love and understanding flow easily today.

Affirmation & Gratitude

"I nurture my relationships with love and care, knowing that strong connections bring joy and fulfillment."

Virgo
26 May 2025

Today Dear Virgo, your analytical nature will shine as you tackle tasks that require focus and precision. Whether you're working on a project at work or organizing your personal life, your attention to detail will lead to success. Today's energy supports logical thinking and careful planning, so don't rush through anything. Take your time to approach each task with care, and you'll feel a sense of accomplishment by the end of the day.

Affirmation & Gratitude

"I trust in my analytical mind to navigate tasks with clarity and precision, leading to success and satisfaction."

 Virgo
27 May 2025

Today Dear Virgo, it's a good day for self-reflection and personal growth. Take some time to think about your goals and the direction you want to take in life. Today's energy supports introspection and planning for the future. Use this time to gain clarity on what matters most to you and make a plan for moving forward. Trust in your inner wisdom to guide your decisions and help you create a fulfilling path.

Affirmation & Gratitude

"I embrace moments of self-reflection, trusting that clarity and personal growth come from within."

Virgo
28 May 2025

Today Dear Virgo, creativity flows easily. Whether you're working on a personal project, solving a problem, or exploring a new idea, today's energy supports innovation and fresh thinking. Don't be afraid to experiment with different approaches or think outside the box. Your imagination will lead you to exciting new possibilities and opportunities. Trust in your creative spirit and let it guide you toward success.

Affirmation & Gratitude

"I embrace my creative spirit, allowing it to guide me toward new ideas and exciting possibilities."

Virgo

29 May 2025

Today Dear Virgo, communication is key. Whether you're resolving a conflict, having important conversations, or simply connecting with others, your ability to express yourself clearly and thoughtfully will lead to positive outcomes. Be open and honest in your communication, and make an effort to listen to others with empathy. By fostering clear and respectful dialogue, you'll strengthen your relationships and build trust. Don't hesitate to address any misunderstandings—today is a day for healing through communication.

Affirmation & Gratitude

"I communicate openly and honestly, trusting that clarity and understanding lead to stronger connections."

 Virgo
30 May 2025

Today Dear Virgo, self-care is essential. You may feel the need to rest and recharge after a busy period. Take time to focus on your well-being, whether through physical rest, emotional nourishment, or simply slowing down. Listen to your body and honor its needs. Today's energy supports healing and renewal, so don't hesitate to take a break from the hustle and bustle. You'll return to your responsibilities feeling refreshed and ready to tackle what's ahead.

Affirmation & Gratitude

"I honor my body's need for rest and renewal, allowing myself to recharge and feel rejuvenated."

 Virgo
31 May 2025

Today Dear Virgo, balance is key. Whether you're juggling work responsibilities or personal obligations, today's energy encourages you to find harmony between your tasks and your well-being. Prioritize your day and make time for rest and relaxation. By maintaining balance, you'll feel more centered and capable of handling whatever comes your way. Trust that balance will lead to peace and productivity. Take time for self-care, and you'll be better equipped to tackle your to-do list.

Affirmation & Gratitude

"I create balance in my life, knowing that harmony between work and rest leads to peace and fulfillment."

June 2025

Virgo
01 June 2025

Today Dear Virgo, creativity abounds, and you're encouraged to think outside the box. Whether you're working on a personal project or finding new solutions to challenges, today's energy supports innovation. Let your imagination take the lead, and don't be afraid to try new approaches. Your unique ideas will open up opportunities that others may not see. Trust in your creative instincts and allow yourself to experiment. Embrace the unknown with confidence and curiosity.

Affirmation & Gratitude

"I embrace my creative spirit, allowing it to guide me toward new ideas and exciting opportunities."

Virgo
02 June 2025

Today Dear Virgo, relationships are in focus, and it's a good day to nurture the connections that matter most to you. Whether through meaningful conversations, acts of kindness, or spending quality time, your efforts will strengthen your bonds. Be present and attentive to the needs of others, and you'll find that your relationships deepen. Love and understanding will flow easily today, bringing harmony and joy to your interactions.

Affirmation & Gratitude

"I nurture my relationships with love and care, knowing that strong connections bring joy and fulfillment."

 Virgo
03 June 2025

Today Dear Virgo, balance is key. You may feel pulled in different directions, but it's important to create harmony between your work and personal life. Take time to prioritize your tasks and ensure that you're giving equal attention to your well-being. By maintaining balance, you'll feel more centered and able to handle your responsibilities with ease. Trust that finding equilibrium will lead to greater peace and productivity.

Affirmation & Gratitude

"I create balance in my life, knowing that harmony between work and rest leads to peace and fulfillment."

Virgo
04 June 2025

Today Dear Virgo, your analytical nature is in full force, making it a great day to tackle complex tasks. Whether at work or in your personal life, your attention to detail and problem-solving abilities will shine. Don't be afraid to dive deep into projects that require precision and focus. Your efforts will lead to success and a sense of accomplishment by the end of the day. Trust in your ability to navigate challenges with clarity and confidence.

Affirmation & Gratitude

"I trust my analytical mind to handle tasks with precision, leading to success and fulfillment."

Virgo

05 June 2025

Today Dear Virgo, communication is essential. Whether you're resolving a conflict, having an important conversation, or simply connecting with others, your ability to express yourself clearly and thoughtfully will lead to positive results. Be open to listening to others and offering your perspective with kindness. By fostering open and honest communication, you'll strengthen your relationships and build trust. Today's energy supports healing through dialogue, so don't hesitate to address any misunderstandings.

Affirmation & Gratitude

"I communicate openly and honestly, trusting that clarity and understanding lead to stronger connections."

 Virgo
06 June 2025

Today Dear Virgo, your focus is on productivity and organization. Whether you're tackling tasks at work or managing your personal life, today's energy supports efficiency and attention to detail. Take advantage of this boost in motivation to complete lingering projects and create a sense of order. Your practical nature will guide you in prioritizing what needs to be done. By the end of the day, you'll feel a sense of accomplishment and satisfaction with your efforts.

Affirmation & Gratitude

"I am focused and productive, trusting that my efforts lead to success and fulfillment."

 Virgo
07 June 2025

Today Dear Virgo, it's a day for self-care and personal well-being. You've been busy lately, and today's energy encourages you to slow down and recharge. Whether through physical rest, emotional nourishment, or simply taking a break from your responsibilities, prioritize your health and well-being. By taking care of yourself, you'll restore your energy and feel more balanced. Don't underestimate the power of rest—it's a vital part of maintaining balance and productivity.

Affirmation & Gratitude

"I honor my body's need for rest and renewal, knowing that self-care is essential for my well-being."

Virgo
08 June 2025

Today Dear Virgo, teamwork is emphasized. Whether you're collaborating on a project or spending time with friends or family, today's energy supports cooperation and shared success. Be open to other people's ideas and contributions, and don't hesitate to offer your own insights. Working together will lead to greater achievements than going it alone. Trust in the power of collaboration and the value of community.

Affirmation & Gratitude

"I am grateful for the power of teamwork, knowing that collaboration leads to shared success and deeper connections."

 Virgo

09 June 2025

Today Dear Virgo, your practical nature will shine as you focus on organizing and planning for the future. Whether it's at work or in your personal life, today's energy supports logical thinking and careful attention to detail. Take the time to create a clear plan for your goals, and don't rush through anything. Your ability to organize and plan will set you up for success. Trust in your practical nature to guide you in making smart decisions.

Affirmation & Gratitude

"I trust my practical nature and attention to detail to guide me toward success and fulfillment."

Virgo
10 June 2025

Today Dear Virgo, balance is essential. You may feel pulled in different directions, but it's important to find harmony between work and relaxation. Take time to prioritize your tasks and focus on what's most important. Don't overextend yourself—remember to make room for self-care and relaxation. By creating balance, you'll feel more centered and capable of handling everything on your plate. Trust that balance leads to peace and productivity.

Affirmation & Gratitude

"I create balance in my life, knowing that harmony between work and rest leads to peace and fulfillment."

 Virgo
11 June 2025

Today Dear Virgo, it's a great day for personal growth and reflection. Take some time to think about where you are in your journey and where you want to go next. Journaling, meditation, or quiet reflection will help you gain insight into your next steps. This is a time for planning and envisioning the future. Don't rush the process—allow yourself space to think deeply about your goals and values.

Affirmation & Gratitude

"I trust my inner wisdom to guide me toward clarity and personal growth."

Virgo
12 June 2025

Today Dear Virgo, creativity is flowing. Whether you're working on a personal project, solving a problem, or exploring a new idea, today's energy supports innovation. Don't be afraid to experiment with different approaches or try something new. Your unique perspective will lead to exciting breakthroughs and fresh opportunities. Trust in your creative abilities and let your imagination guide you toward success.

Affirmation & Gratitude

"I embrace my creative spirit, allowing it to guide me toward new ideas and exciting opportunities."

 # Virgo
13 June 2025

Today Dear Virgo, relationships take center stage. It's a good day to strengthen your bonds with loved ones and express your appreciation for the people who matter most. Whether through quality time, thoughtful gestures, or open conversations, your efforts will deepen your connections and bring joy to your relationships. Be present and attentive, and you'll find that love and understanding flow easily today.

Affirmation & Gratitude

"I nurture my relationships with love and care, knowing that strong connections bring joy and fulfillment."

♍ Virgo
14 June 2025

Today Dear Virgo, your analytical nature will shine as you tackle tasks that require focus and precision. Whether you're working on a project at work or organizing your personal life, your attention to detail will lead to success. Today's energy supports logical thinking and careful planning, so don't rush through anything. Take your time to approach each task with care, and you'll feel a sense of accomplishment by the end of the day.

Affirmation & Gratitude

"I trust in my analytical mind to navigate tasks with clarity and precision, leading to success and satisfaction."

Virgo

15 June 2025

Today Dear Virgo, it's a good day for self-reflection and personal growth. Take some time to think about your goals and the direction you want to take in life. Today's energy supports introspection and planning for the future. Use this time to gain clarity on what matters most to you and make a plan for moving forward. Trust in your inner wisdom to guide your decisions and help you create a fulfilling path.

Affirmation & Gratitude

"I embrace moments of self-reflection, trusting that clarity and personal growth come from within."

Virgo
16 June 2025

Today Dear Virgo, your creativity is in full bloom. Whether you're working on a personal project, solving a problem, or exploring a new idea, today's energy supports thinking outside the box. Don't be afraid to experiment with different approaches or explore new possibilities. Your imagination will lead you to exciting breakthroughs and new opportunities. Trust in your creative spirit and let it guide you toward success.

Affirmation & Gratitude

"I embrace my creative spirit, allowing it to lead me toward new ideas and exciting opportunities."

 Virgo
17 June 2025

Today Dear Virgo, your focus turns to relationships. Whether it's deepening a romantic connection, spending time with family, or nurturing friendships, today's energy supports strengthening your bonds with others. Make an effort to show appreciation for the people who matter most to you, and don't hesitate to reach out and express your feelings. Meaningful conversations and acts of kindness will go a long way in deepening your connections.

Affirmation & Gratitude

"I nurture my relationships with love and care, knowing that strong connections bring joy and fulfillment."

 Virgo
18 June 2025

Today Dear Virgo, balance is essential. You may be juggling multiple responsibilities, but it's important to find harmony between work and personal life. Today's energy supports creating structure and prioritizing your tasks. Focus on what's most important and don't hesitate to delegate or let go of anything that's no longer serving you. By achieving balance, you'll feel more centered and able to handle your day with ease. Trust that balance leads to peace and fulfillment.

Affirmation & Gratitude

"I create balance in my life, knowing that harmony between work and rest brings peace and fulfillment."

 Virgo
19 June 2025

Today Dear Virgo, communication is key. Whether you're resolving conflicts, having important conversations, or simply connecting with others, your ability to express yourself clearly and thoughtfully will lead to positive outcomes. Be open and honest in your communication, and make an effort to listen to others with empathy. By fostering clear and respectful dialogue, you'll strengthen your relationships and build trust. Don't hesitate to address any misunderstandings—today is a day for healing through communication.

Affirmation & Gratitude

"I communicate openly and honestly, trusting that clarity and understanding lead to stronger connections."

♍ Virgo
20 June 2025

Today Dear Virgo, teamwork is emphasized. Whether you're collaborating on a work project or spending time with friends and family, today's energy supports cooperation and shared success. Be open to other people's ideas and contributions, and don't hesitate to offer your own insights. Working together will lead to greater achievements than going it alone. Trust in the power of collaboration and the value of community.

Affirmation & Gratitude

"I am grateful for the power of collaboration, knowing that shared efforts lead to greater success and stronger connections."

 Virgo
21 June 2025

Today Dear Virgo, your practical nature is in high demand. Whether you're managing a project, organizing your home, or planning for the future, today's energy supports logical thinking and careful attention to detail. Take the time to approach tasks methodically and ensure that everything is in order. Your ability to plan and organize will lead to success and a sense of accomplishment. Trust in your practical skills to navigate challenges and achieve your goals.

Affirmation & Gratitude

"I trust in my practical nature and attention to detail to guide me toward success and accomplishment."

Virgo

22 June 2025

Today Dear Virgo, your focus turns inward, and it's a good day for introspection. Spend some time reflecting on your goals and values, and think about where you're headed in life. Journaling, meditation, or simply quiet reflection will help you gain clarity and insight. This is a time for deep thinking and self-awareness, so don't rush through the process. Allow yourself the space to consider your next steps with care and intention.

Affirmation & Gratitude

"I trust my inner voice to guide me toward clarity and self-awareness."

 Virgo
23 June 2025

Today Dear Virgo, your attention to detail will be a valuable asset. Whether at work or home, today's energy supports organization and precision. Focus on completing tasks that require careful attention, and take your time to ensure everything is done correctly. Your meticulous nature will help you achieve high-quality results, and others will appreciate your thoroughness. Don't rush through anything today—allow yourself the time to produce the best possible outcome.

Affirmation & Gratitude

"I take pride in my attention to detail, knowing that it leads to excellence and success in all I do."

 Virgo
24 June 2025

Today Dear Virgo, creativity flows easily. Whether you're working on a personal project, solving a problem, or exploring new ideas, today's energy supports innovation and fresh thinking. Don't be afraid to experiment with different approaches or think outside the box. Your imagination will lead you to exciting new possibilities and opportunities. Trust in your creative spirit and let it guide you toward success.

Affirmation & Gratitude

"I embrace my creative spirit, allowing it to guide me toward new ideas and exciting possibilities."

 Virgo
25 June 2025

Today Dear Virgo, balance is key. Whether you're juggling work responsibilities or personal obligations, today's energy encourages you to find harmony between your tasks and your well-being. Prioritize your day and make time for rest and relaxation. By maintaining balance, you'll feel more centered and capable of handling whatever comes your way. Trust that balance will lead to peace and productivity. Take time for self-care, and you'll be better equipped to tackle your to-do list.

Affirmation & Gratitude

"I create balance in my life, knowing that harmony between work and rest leads to peace and fulfillment."

 Virgo
26 June 2025

Today Dear Virgo, self-care is essential. You may feel the need to rest and recharge after a busy period. Take time to focus on your well-being, whether through physical rest, emotional nourishment, or simply slowing down. Listen to your body and honor its needs. Today's energy supports healing and renewal, so don't hesitate to take a break from the hustle and bustle. You'll return to your responsibilities feeling refreshed and ready to tackle what's ahead.

Affirmation & Gratitude

"I honor my body's need for rest and renewal, allowing myself to recharge and feel rejuvenated."

# Virgo
27 June 2025

Today Dear Virgo, communication is key. Whether you're resolving a conflict, having important conversations, or simply connecting with others, your ability to express yourself clearly and thoughtfully will lead to positive outcomes. Be open to listening to others and offering your perspective with kindness. By fostering open and honest communication, you'll strengthen your relationships and build trust. Today's energy supports healing through dialogue, so don't hesitate to address any misunderstandings.

Affirmation & Gratitude

"I communicate openly and honestly, trusting that clarity and understanding lead to stronger connections."

 Virgo
28 June 2025

Today Dear Virgo, your focus is on productivity and organization. Whether you're tackling tasks at work or managing your personal life, today's energy supports efficiency and attention to detail. Take advantage of this boost in motivation to complete lingering projects and create a sense of order. Your practical nature will guide you in prioritizing what needs to be done. By the end of the day, you'll feel a sense of accomplishment and satisfaction with your efforts.

Affirmation & Gratitude

"I am focused and productive, trusting that my efforts lead to success and fulfillment."

 Virgo
29 June 2025

Today Dear Virgo, relationships take center stage. Whether with friends, family, or romantic partners, today is a good day to nurture your connections. Reach out to someone you care about, offer a helping hand, or simply spend quality time together. Strengthening your bonds will bring joy and fulfillment. Open your heart to love and understanding, and you'll find that your relationships deepen and grow stronger.

Affirmation & Gratitude

"I nurture my relationships with love and care, knowing that strong connections bring joy and fulfillment."

♍ Virgo
30 June 2025

Today Dear Virgo, it's a great day for learning and expanding your knowledge. Whether you're diving into a new subject, reading, or taking a course, today's energy supports intellectual growth. Allow yourself to be curious and explore topics that pique your interest. The knowledge you gain today will serve you well in the future and open up new opportunities for personal and professional growth. Embrace the joy of learning and trust that your curiosity will lead you in the right direction.

Affirmation & Gratitude

"I am grateful for my curiosity and the opportunities for learning that help me grow and evolve."

July 2025

 Virgo
01 July 2025

Today Dear Virgo, it's a day to focus on new beginnings. Whether you're starting a new project, setting fresh goals, or adopting a new mindset, today's energy supports growth and transformation. Be open to opportunities and embrace change with confidence. This is a time to plant seeds for your future success, so set clear intentions and take proactive steps forward. Trust that you're on the right path and that everything is aligning to help you achieve your goals.

Affirmation & Gratitude

"I embrace new beginnings with confidence, trusting that each step leads me toward growth and fulfillment."

Virgo
02 July 2025

Today Dear Virgo, communication is key. Whether you're resolving a conflict or having an important conversation, clear and thoughtful expression will lead to positive outcomes. Be open to listening and offering your perspective with empathy. Today's energy supports healing through dialogue, so don't hesitate to address any misunderstandings. By fostering respectful communication, you'll strengthen your relationships and build trust. Approach conversations with kindness and patience.

Affirmation & Gratitude

"I communicate openly and kindly, trusting that clarity and understanding lead to stronger and more trusting connections."

 Virgo
03 July 2025

Today Dear Virgo, your analytical mind is sharp, making it a great day to tackle complex tasks. Whether at work or in your personal life, your attention to detail and logical thinking will guide you to success. Don't be afraid to dive into projects that require focus and precision. Your efforts will pay off, and you'll feel a sense of accomplishment by the day's end. Trust in your problem-solving abilities and embrace the challenges that come your way.

Affirmation & Gratitude

"I trust my analytical mind to approach tasks with clarity and precision, leading to success and fulfillment."

Virgo
04 July 2025

Today Dear Virgo, balance is essential. You may feel pulled in different directions, but it's important to create harmony between work and relaxation. Prioritize your tasks and focus on what's most important, but don't forget to take care of yourself along the way. By maintaining balance, you'll feel more grounded and capable of handling your responsibilities with ease. Make space for rest and relaxation today, and trust that balance will lead to peace and productivity.

Affirmation & Gratitude

"I create balance in my life, knowing that harmony between work and rest leads to inner peace and fulfillment."

 Virgo
05 July 2025

Today Dear Virgo, relationships take center stage. Whether you're nurturing a romantic connection, deepening a friendship, or spending time with family, today is a great day to strengthen your bonds. Be present with those you care about and show appreciation for the love and support they offer. Meaningful conversations and thoughtful gestures will bring joy to your relationships and deepen your connections. Open your heart and express your feelings with kindness.

Affirmation & Gratitude

"I nurture my relationships with love and care, knowing that strong connections bring joy and fulfillment."

Virgo
06 July 2025

Today Dear Virgo, creativity flows easily. Whether you're working on a personal project, exploring a new idea, or finding fresh solutions to challenges, today's energy supports innovation. Don't be afraid to experiment with different approaches or think outside the box. Your unique perspective will lead to exciting breakthroughs and new opportunities. Trust in your creative abilities and let your imagination guide you toward success. Embrace the unknown and explore the possibilities that come your way.

Affirmation & Gratitude

"I embrace my creative spirit, allowing it to guide me toward new ideas and exciting opportunities."

 Virgo
07 July 2025

Today Dear Virgo, your focus turns to productivity and organization. Whether you're managing your responsibilities at work or taking care of tasks at home, today's energy supports efficiency. Make a plan, prioritize your tasks, and follow through with care and attention to detail. By staying organized, you'll feel accomplished by the end of the day. Don't rush through anything—take your time to ensure quality in all you do. Your practical nature will guide you to success.

Affirmation & Gratitude

"I am focused and productive, trusting that my efforts today lead to success and fulfillment."

Virgo
08 July 2025

Today Dear Virgo, it's a day for introspection and reflection. Take some time to think about your goals, values, and the direction you want to take in life. Today's energy supports deep thinking and planning for the future. Use this time to gain clarity on what matters most to you and how you can align your actions with your true desires. Journaling or meditation will help you connect with your inner wisdom and find the clarity you seek.

Affirmation & Gratitude

"I honor moments of self-reflection, trusting that inner wisdom leads to clarity and personal growth."

Virgo

09 July 2025

Today Dear Virgo, teamwork is emphasized. Whether you're working on a project with colleagues or spending time with friends and family, today's energy supports collaboration and shared success. Be open to other people's ideas and contributions, and don't hesitate to offer your own insights. Working together will lead to greater achievements than you could accomplish alone. Trust in the power of collaboration and the value of community, and embrace the support that others offer.

Affirmation & Gratitude

"I am grateful for the power of teamwork, knowing that shared efforts lead to greater success and stronger connections."

Virgo
10 July 2025

Today Dear Virgo, your practical side is highlighted. Whether you're organizing your space, managing your schedule, or tackling a big project, today's energy supports logical thinking and attention to detail. Take the time to approach tasks methodically and ensure that everything is in order. By staying focused and practical, you'll achieve positive results and feel a sense of accomplishment by the end of the day. Trust in your ability to organize and plan effectively, and success will follow.

Affirmation & Gratitude

"I trust my practical nature and attention to detail to guide me toward success and accomplishment."

Virgo
11 July 2025

Today Dear Virgo, self-care is essential. You may feel the need to rest and recharge after a busy period. Take time to focus on your well-being, whether through physical rest, emotional nourishment, or simply slowing down. Today's energy supports healing and renewal, so don't hesitate to take a break from the hustle and bustle. You'll return to your responsibilities feeling refreshed and ready to tackle what's ahead with clarity and renewed energy.

Affirmation & Gratitude

"I honor my body's need for rest and renewal, allowing myself to recharge and feel rejuvenated."

Virgo
12 July 2025

Today Dear Virgo, communication is key. Whether you're resolving a conflict, having important conversations, or simply connecting with others, your ability to express yourself clearly and thoughtfully will lead to positive outcomes. Be open to listening to others and offering your perspective with kindness. By fostering open and honest communication, you'll strengthen your relationships and build trust. Don't hesitate to address any misunderstandings—today is a day for healing through dialogue.

Affirmation & Gratitude

"I communicate openly and honestly, trusting that clarity and understanding lead to stronger connections."

Virgo

13 July 2025

Today Dear Virgo, creativity is flowing. Whether you're working on a personal project, solving a problem, or exploring a new idea, today's energy supports thinking outside the box. Don't be afraid to experiment with different approaches or explore new possibilities. Your unique perspective will help you find innovative solutions and opportunities that others might overlook. Trust in your creative abilities and let your imagination guide you toward success. Embrace the excitement of new ideas.

Affirmation & Gratitude

"I embrace my creative spirit, allowing it to guide me toward new ideas and exciting opportunities."

♍ Virgo
14 July 2025

Today Dear Virgo, relationships are highlighted. Whether you're spending time with loved ones, reconnecting with friends, or deepening a romantic connection, today's energy supports nurturing your bonds. Be present and attentive in your interactions, and show appreciation for the people who bring joy and support into your life. Acts of kindness, love, and understanding will strengthen your relationships and create harmony. Don't be afraid to express your feelings openly and build deeper connections.

Affirmation & Gratitude

"I nurture my relationships with love and care, knowing that strong connections bring joy and fulfillment."

Virgo

15 July 2025

Today Dear Virgo, balance is key. You may feel the need to balance your work with personal time. Take the time to evaluate your priorities and create a daily routine that supports both your responsibilities and your well-being. By achieving balance, you'll feel more centered and able to handle the demands of the day with ease. Make sure to create space for relaxation and personal enjoyment to recharge and stay grounded.

Affirmation & Gratitude

"I create balance in my life, knowing that harmony between work and rest brings peace and fulfillment."

Virgo
16 July 2025

Today Dear Virgo, your attention to detail is your greatest asset today. Whether you're working on a project at work or organizing your personal life, your meticulous nature will help you achieve success. Focus on the finer details, and take your time to ensure that everything is done correctly. Your careful planning and thoughtful approach will lead to positive outcomes. Don't rush through anything—embrace your methodical approach, and you'll feel a sense of accomplishment by the end of the day.

Affirmation & Gratitude

"I take pride in my attention to detail, knowing that it leads to excellence and success in all I do."

Virgo

17 July 2025

Today Dear Virgo, your creative energy is strong. Whether you're working on a personal project, solving a problem, or exploring new ideas, today's energy supports thinking outside the box. Don't be afraid to try new approaches or experiment with different methods. Your innovative thinking will lead to breakthroughs and fresh opportunities. Trust in your creative abilities, and let your imagination guide you toward new and exciting possibilities. Today is a great day to embrace your creativity and let it flow freely.

Affirmation & Gratitude

"I embrace my creative spirit, allowing it to guide me toward new ideas and exciting opportunities."

Virgo

18 July 2025

Today Dear Virgo, communication is key to success. Whether at work or in your personal life, your ability to express yourself clearly and thoughtfully will lead to positive outcomes. Be open to listening to others and offer your perspective with empathy. Honest and open communication will build trust and strengthen your relationships. Don't shy away from difficult conversations—today's energy supports healing through dialogue. Approach every conversation with kindness and clarity, and you'll find understanding and resolution.

Affirmation & Gratitude

"I communicate openly and honestly, trusting that clarity and understanding lead to stronger and more meaningful connections."

Virgo

19 July 2025

Today Dear Virgo, it's a great day to focus on your personal well-being. Self-care is essential, and today's energy encourages you to prioritize your health and happiness. Whether through physical rest, emotional nourishment, or mental relaxation, take time to recharge your energy. By giving yourself the care and attention you need, you'll feel refreshed and ready to tackle the days ahead. Don't feel guilty about taking time for yourself—self-care is vital to your overall well-being.

Affirmation & Gratitude

"I honor my body's need for rest and renewal, knowing that self-care is essential for my well-being."

Virgo
20 July 2025

Today Dear Virgo, teamwork is emphasized. Whether you're working with colleagues, family, or friends, today's energy supports collaboration and shared success. Be open to listening to others and offer your insights. Together, you can achieve greater results than working alone. Trust in the power of teamwork and the strength that comes from supporting one another. Today is a reminder that cooperation leads to mutual success and deeper connections.

Affirmation & Gratitude

"I am grateful for the power of teamwork, knowing that shared efforts lead to greater success and stronger connections."

 # Virgo
21 July 2025

Today Dear Virgo, your practical nature is highlighted. Today's energy supports planning, organizing, and attention to detail. Whether you're managing a project or preparing for the future, your logical thinking and careful approach will set you up for success. Don't rush through anything—take the time to ensure that all the details are in place. Trust in your ability to plan and execute with precision. Your hard work will lead to positive outcomes and a sense of accomplishment.

Affirmation & Gratitude

"I trust my practical nature and attention to detail to guide me toward success and accomplishment."

Virgo
22 July 2025

Today Dear Virgo, self-reflection and introspection are essential. Take some quiet time to reflect on your personal journey and the goals you've set for yourself. Are you aligned with your true desires? Today's energy encourages you to assess where you are and where you want to go. Trust in your inner wisdom to guide your decisions and make any necessary adjustments. By taking time to reflect, you'll gain clarity and insight into your next steps.

Affirmation & Gratitude

"I honor moments of self-reflection, trusting that inner wisdom leads to clarity and personal growth."

# Virgo
23 July 2025

Today Dear Virgo, your creative energy is in full swing. Whether you're working on a personal project, solving problems, or exploring new ideas, today's energy supports innovation and fresh perspectives. Don't hesitate to think outside the box and experiment with new approaches. Your creative thinking will lead to breakthroughs and exciting opportunities. Trust in your ability to see things from a unique perspective, and let your creativity guide you toward success.

Affirmation & Gratitude

"I embrace my creative spirit, allowing it to guide me toward new ideas and exciting possibilities."

Virgo
24 July 2025

Today Dear Virgo, your relationships are in focus. Whether you're connecting with loved ones, deepening friendships, or nurturing romantic bonds, today's energy supports love and harmony. Be present with the people who matter most, and show appreciation for the joy they bring to your life. Meaningful conversations and acts of kindness will strengthen your relationships and create lasting bonds. Open your heart to love and connection, and you'll find that your relationships grow even stronger.

Affirmation & Gratitude

"I nurture my relationships with love and care, knowing that strong connections bring joy and fulfillment."

 Virgo
25 July 2025

Today Dear Virgo, balance is key. You may feel pulled in different directions, but it's important to create harmony between work and personal life. Today's energy supports creating structure and prioritizing your tasks. Focus on what's most important and don't hesitate to delegate or let go of anything that's no longer serving you. By achieving balance, you'll feel more centered and able to handle your day with ease. Trust that balance leads to peace and fulfillment.

Affirmation & Gratitude

"I create balance in my life, knowing that harmony between work and rest brings peace and fulfillment."

Virgo
26 July 2025

Today Dear Virgo, your analytical mind will shine. Today's energy supports logical thinking and problem-solving, making it a great day to tackle tasks that require focus and attention to detail. Don't be afraid to dive deep into your work and address any challenges head-on. Your ability to break down complex issues and find practical solutions will lead to success. Trust in your analytical skills, and don't hesitate to apply them to any situation that requires a thoughtful approach.

Affirmation & Gratitude

"I trust my analytical mind to navigate challenges with clarity and focus, leading to success and fulfillment."

 # Virgo
27 July 2025

Today Dear Virgo, communication is highlighted. Whether at work or in your personal life, your ability to express yourself clearly and thoughtfully will lead to positive outcomes. Today's energy supports honest conversations and open dialogue. Be open to listening to others, and approach conversations with empathy and understanding. By fostering respectful communication, you'll strengthen your relationships and build trust. Don't hesitate to address any unresolved issues—today is a good day for healing through dialogue.

Affirmation & Gratitude

"I communicate openly and honestly, trusting that clarity and understanding lead to stronger and healthier connections."

Virgo

28 July 2025

Today Dear Virgo, it's a great day for personal growth and self-reflection. Take some time to think about your goals, values, and the direction you're headed in life. Today's energy supports deep thinking and introspection, so use this time to evaluate where you are and what adjustments you'd like to make. Journaling, meditation, or simply quiet reflection will help you gain clarity. Trust in your inner wisdom to guide your next steps, and allow yourself to make the changes needed for a fulfilling journey.

Affirmation & Gratitude

"I embrace moments of self-reflection, trusting that clarity and personal growth come from within."

 Virgo
29 July 2025

Today Dear Virgo, creativity is in the air. Whether you're working on a project, solving a problem, or exploring new ideas, today's energy supports thinking outside the box. Don't be afraid to experiment with different approaches or explore new possibilities. Your unique perspective will help you discover exciting breakthroughs and opportunities that others might miss. Trust in your creative spirit and let it lead you toward innovative solutions and fresh ideas.

Affirmation & Gratitude

"I embrace my creative spirit, allowing it to guide me toward new ideas and exciting possibilities."

Virgo
30 July 2025

Today Dear Virgo, balance is important. You may feel pulled between work and personal obligations, but it's essential to create harmony in your day. Prioritize your tasks and ensure that you're giving equal attention to your well-being. By maintaining balance, you'll feel more centered and ready to handle your responsibilities with ease. Make time for self-care and relaxation, and you'll find that you're more productive and focused. Trust that balance leads to peace and fulfillment.

Affirmation & Gratitude

"I create balance in my life, knowing that harmony between work and rest leads to peace and fulfillment."

 Virgo
31 July 2025

Today Dear Virgo, relationships take center stage. It's a good day to nurture your connections with loved ones and express your appreciation for the people who bring joy to your life. Whether through quality time, thoughtful gestures, or open conversations, your efforts will deepen your relationships and create lasting bonds. Be present and attentive in your interactions, and you'll find that love and understanding flow easily today. Open your heart and connect with those who matter most.

Affirmation & Gratitude

"I nurture my relationships with love and care, knowing that strong connections bring joy and fulfillment."

August 2025

Virgo

01 August 2025

Today Dear Virgo, it's a great day to focus on self-care and personal well-being. Whether it's physical rest, emotional healing, or mental relaxation, today's energy supports slowing down and recharging. By nurturing yourself, you'll restore your energy and be better equipped to handle the demands of daily life. Don't feel guilty for taking time for yourself—self-care is essential for maintaining balance and overall health. Prioritize your well-being today and trust that by taking care of yourself, you'll be able to give more to others.

Affirmation & Gratitude

"I honor my body's need for rest and renewal, knowing that self-care is essential for my well-being."

Virgo
02 August 2025

Today Dear Virgo, your creative energy is flowing, making it a perfect day to work on personal projects or explore new ideas. Whether you're tackling a creative challenge or simply finding new solutions, today's energy supports innovation and outside-the-box thinking. Don't hesitate to experiment with different approaches—your imagination will lead to exciting breakthroughs and fresh opportunities. Trust in your creative abilities, and allow your curiosity to guide you toward success. Embrace the freedom of creative expression and the possibilities it brings.

Affirmation & Gratitude

"I embrace my creative spirit, allowing it to guide me toward new ideas and exciting possibilities."

Virgo
03 August 2025

Today Dear Virgo, communication is key. Whether you're resolving misunderstandings, having important conversations, or simply connecting with others, your ability to express yourself clearly and thoughtfully will lead to positive results. Be open to hearing others' perspectives and offering your insights with empathy. Today's energy supports healing and growth through dialogue, so don't shy away from addressing unresolved issues. By fostering clear communication, you'll strengthen your relationships and build trust. Approach all conversations with kindness and clarity.

Affirmation & Gratitude

"I communicate openly and kindly, trusting that clarity and understanding lead to stronger connections and healing."

Virgo
04 August 2025

Today Dear Virgo, balance is essential. You may feel pulled between responsibilities at work and personal obligations, but it's important to create harmony between the two. Focus on prioritizing tasks and making time for self-care. Don't spread yourself too thin—remember that balance is key to maintaining your well-being and staying productive. By creating structure and making time for relaxation, you'll be more centered and capable of handling whatever the day brings. Trust that balance will lead to peace and fulfillment.

Affirmation & Gratitude

"I create balance in my life, knowing that harmony between work and rest leads to peace and fulfillment."

Virgo
05 August 2025

Today Dear Virgo, your attention to detail will shine. Whether you're working on a project, managing your daily tasks, or organizing your space, today's energy supports precision and careful planning. Take your time to ensure that everything is in order and don't rush through anything. Your practical nature and focus on the finer points will lead to success and a sense of accomplishment by the end of the day. Trust in your ability to navigate tasks with clarity and precision.

Affirmation & Gratitude

"I take pride in my attention to detail, knowing that it leads to excellence and success in all I do."

Virgo
06 August 2025

Today Dear Virgo, relationships are highlighted, and today is a great day to strengthen your connections with loved ones. Whether through meaningful conversations, thoughtful gestures, or simply spending quality time together, your efforts to nurture your relationships will be rewarded. Be present and attentive in your interactions, and show appreciation for the people who bring joy to your life. Love and understanding will flow easily today, deepening your bonds and creating harmony in your relationships.

Affirmation & Gratitude

"I nurture my relationships with love and care, knowing that strong connections bring joy and fulfillment."

Virgo
07 August 2025

Today Dear Virgo, creativity is in full bloom. Whether you're working on a personal project, solving a problem, or exploring new ideas, today's energy supports innovative thinking. Don't be afraid to experiment with new approaches or try something different. Your imagination will lead you to exciting breakthroughs and fresh opportunities. Trust in your creative spirit and let it guide you toward success. Embrace the excitement that comes from thinking outside the box and exploring new possibilities.

Affirmation & Gratitude

"I embrace my creative spirit, allowing it to guide me toward new ideas and exciting opportunities."

Virgo
08 August 2025

Today Dear Virgo, teamwork is emphasized. Whether you're collaborating on a project at work, engaging with friends, or spending time with family, today's energy supports cooperation and shared success. Be open to listening to others and offering your insights. By working together, you'll achieve more than you could alone. Trust in the power of collaboration, and embrace the support and contributions of those around you. Teamwork will lead to greater accomplishments and deeper connections.

Affirmation & Gratitude

"I am grateful for the power of teamwork, knowing that collaboration leads to shared success and deeper connections."

Virgo

09 August 2025

Today Dear Virgo, your focus turns to organization and planning. Whether you're managing a project, organizing your home, or setting long-term goals, today's energy supports logical thinking and attention to detail. Take the time to carefully plan out your day or week, and don't rush through anything. Your practical nature will help you stay on track and achieve your objectives. Trust that your ability to plan and organize will lead to success and a sense of accomplishment.

Affirmation & Gratitude

"I trust my practical nature and attention to detail to guide me toward success and fulfillment."

Virgo
10 August 2025

Today Dear Virgo, balance is key. You may be juggling multiple responsibilities, but it's important to find harmony between work and personal life. Prioritize your tasks, but also make time for relaxation and self-care. By maintaining balance, you'll feel more grounded and capable of handling the demands of the day. Remember that balance is essential for both your productivity and your well-being. Take the time to create a routine that supports both your goals and your personal happiness.

Affirmation & Gratitude

"I create balance in my life, knowing that harmony between work and rest leads to peace and fulfillment."

 Virgo
11 August 2025

Today Dear Virgo, creativity is your ally. Whether you're working on a personal project, brainstorming ideas, or tackling a challenge, today's energy supports thinking outside the box. Don't be afraid to try new approaches and experiment with different methods. Your innovative thinking will lead to breakthroughs and fresh solutions that others might overlook. Trust in your ability to see things from a unique perspective, and let your imagination guide you toward success.

Affirmation & Gratitude

"I embrace my creative spirit, allowing it to guide me toward new ideas and exciting possibilities."

Virgo
12 August 2025

Today Dear Virgo, communication is highlighted. Whether you're resolving a conflict, having important conversations, or simply connecting with others, your ability to express yourself clearly and thoughtfully will lead to positive outcomes. Be open to listening to others and offering your perspective with empathy. By fostering honest and respectful dialogue, you'll strengthen your relationships and build trust. Don't hesitate to address any unresolved issues—today is a great day for healing through communication.

Affirmation & Gratitude

"I communicate openly and honestly, trusting that clarity and understanding lead to stronger and healthier connections."

 Virgo
13 August 2025

Today Dear Virgo, your focus turns inward, and it's a good day for introspection and personal growth. Take some quiet time to reflect on your goals and values, and think about where you're headed in life. Journaling, meditation, or quiet reflection will help you gain clarity and insight into your next steps. This is a time for deep thinking and self-awareness, so allow yourself the space to consider your path with care and intention.

Affirmation & Gratitude

"I trust my inner wisdom to guide me toward clarity and personal growth."

Virgo
14 August 2025

Today Dear Virgo, balance is important. Whether you're managing work responsibilities or personal commitments, today's energy encourages you to create harmony in your day. Focus on prioritizing what's most important, but don't forget to take time for self-care and relaxation. By finding balance, you'll feel more centered and capable of handling everything on your plate. Trust that balance leads to both peace and productivity. Take care of yourself, and you'll be able to give your best in all areas of your life.

Affirmation & Gratitude

"I create balance in my life, knowing that harmony between work and rest leads to peace and fulfillment."

Virgo
15 August 2025

Today Dear Virgo, your analytical mind is your greatest strength today. Whether you're working on a project that requires precision, solving a problem, or organizing your space, your attention to detail will lead to success. Take your time to ensure that everything is done correctly, and don't rush through anything. Your practical approach and logical thinking will help you navigate challenges with clarity and focus. Trust in your problem-solving abilities, and you'll feel a sense of accomplishment by the end of the day.

Affirmation & Gratitude

"I trust my analytical mind to navigate challenges with clarity and focus, leading to success and fulfillment."

 Virgo
16 August 2025

Today Dear Virgo, relationships take center stage. Whether you're spending time with family, reconnecting with friends, or deepening a romantic connection, today's energy supports love and harmony. Be present and attentive with those who matter most to you, and show appreciation for the joy and support they bring into your life. Thoughtful conversations and acts of kindness will strengthen your bonds and create lasting connections. Open your heart to love and understanding, and your relationships will flourish.

Affirmation & Gratitude

"I nurture my relationships with love and care, knowing that strong connections bring joy and fulfillment."

Virgo
17 August 2025

Today Dear Virgo, creativity is in the air. Whether you're working on a personal project, exploring new ideas, or finding innovative solutions to challenges, today's energy supports fresh thinking. Don't hesitate to experiment with different approaches or think outside the box. Your unique perspective will lead to exciting breakthroughs and new opportunities. Trust in your creative abilities, and let your imagination guide you toward success. Embrace the freedom of creative expression and enjoy the possibilities that come with it.

Affirmation & Gratitude

"I embrace my creative spirit, allowing it to guide me toward new ideas and exciting opportunities."

Virgo
18 August 2025

Today Dear Virgo, communication is essential. Whether at work, in your personal life, or in resolving conflicts, your ability to express yourself clearly and thoughtfully will lead to positive outcomes. Be open to listening to others and offering your perspective with empathy. Honest and open communication will build trust and strengthen your relationships. Don't shy away from important conversations—today is a great day to foster understanding and connection through dialogue.

Affirmation & Gratitude

"I communicate openly and kindly, trusting that clarity and understanding lead to stronger connections and healing."

 Virgo
19 August 2025

Today Dear Virgo, balance is key. You may feel pulled in different directions by your responsibilities, but it's important to find harmony between work and relaxation. Take time to prioritize your tasks and make room for self-care. By maintaining balance, you'll feel more grounded and capable of handling the demands of the day. Trust that balance will lead to both productivity and peace. Take time for yourself today, and you'll find that everything falls into place.

Affirmation & Gratitude

"I create balance in my life, knowing that harmony between work and rest leads to peace and fulfillment."

Virgo
20 August 2025

Today Dear Virgo, your practical nature is your ally. Whether you're organizing your space, managing a project, or planning for the future, today's energy supports logical thinking and attention to detail. Take the time to carefully plan and prioritize your tasks, and don't rush through anything. Your ability to stay organized and focused will lead to success and a sense of accomplishment. Trust in your practical approach to guide you toward positive outcomes, and take pride in your efforts today.

Affirmation & Gratitude

"I trust my practical nature and attention to detail to guide me toward success and fulfillment."

Virgo
21 August 2025

Today Dear Virgo, teamwork is emphasized. Whether you're collaborating with colleagues, friends, or family, today's energy supports cooperation and shared success. Be open to listening to others and offering your insights. Together, you'll achieve more than you could alone. Trust in the power of collaboration, and embrace the support of those around you. Teamwork will lead to greater accomplishments and deeper connections. Celebrate the joy of working together toward common goals.

Affirmation & Gratitude

"I am grateful for the power of teamwork, knowing that collaboration leads to shared success and deeper connections."

Virgo
22 August 2025

Today Dear Virgo, self-care is essential. You've been working hard, and today's energy encourages you to slow down and focus on your well-being. Whether through physical rest, emotional nourishment, or simply taking time to relax, prioritize your health and happiness today. By taking care of yourself, you'll restore your energy and feel more balanced. Don't underestimate the importance of self-care—it's a vital part of maintaining both productivity and peace of mind.

Affirmation & Gratitude

"I honor my body's need for rest and renewal, knowing that self-care is essential for my well-being."

Virgo
23 August 2025

Today Dear Virgo, your creative energy is strong. Whether you're working on a personal project, exploring new ideas, or finding innovative solutions to challenges, today's energy supports thinking outside the box. Don't hesitate to experiment with different approaches or explore new possibilities. Your unique perspective will lead to exciting breakthroughs and new opportunities. Trust in your creative abilities, and let your imagination guide you toward success. Embrace the freedom of creative expression.

Affirmation & Gratitude

"I embrace my creative spirit, allowing it to guide me toward new ideas and exciting opportunities."

Virgo
24 August 2025

Today Dear Virgo, relationships take center stage. Whether you're connecting with loved ones, deepening friendships, or nurturing romantic bonds, today's energy supports love and harmony. Be present with the people who matter most, and show appreciation for the joy they bring into your life. Meaningful conversations and acts of kindness will strengthen your relationships and create lasting bonds. Open your heart to love and connection, and your relationships will flourish.

Affirmation & Gratitude

"I nurture my relationships with love and care, knowing that strong connections bring joy and fulfillment."

# Virgo
25 August 2025

Today Dear Virgo, communication is key. Whether you're resolving conflicts, having important conversations, or simply connecting with others, your ability to express yourself clearly and thoughtfully will lead to positive results. Be open to listening to others and offering your perspective with empathy. By fostering clear and respectful communication, you'll strengthen your relationships and build trust. Don't hesitate to address any misunderstandings—today is a day for healing through dialogue.

Affirmation & Gratitude

"I communicate openly and kindly, trusting that clarity and understanding lead to stronger connections and healing."

Virgo
26 August 2025

Today Dear Virgo, balance is essential. Whether you're juggling responsibilities at work or personal commitments, today's energy encourages you to create harmony in your day. Focus on prioritizing what's most important, but don't forget to take time for self-care and relaxation. By finding balance, you'll feel more centered and capable of handling everything on your plate. Trust that balance leads to peace and fulfillment. Take care of yourself, and you'll be better equipped to give your best in all areas of your life.

Affirmation & Gratitude

"I create balance in my life, knowing that harmony between work and rest leads to peace and fulfillment."

Virgo
27 August 2025

Today Dear Virgo, your attention to detail is a valuable asset today. Whether you're working on a project at work or organizing your personal life, your focus on precision will lead to success. Take your time to ensure that everything is done correctly, and don't rush through any tasks. Your meticulous nature will help you achieve high-quality results, and others will appreciate your thoroughness. Trust in your ability to handle tasks with clarity and care, and you'll feel a sense of accomplishment by the end of the day.

Affirmation & Gratitude

"I take pride in my attention to detail, knowing that it leads to excellence and success in all I do."

Virgo
28 August 2025

Today Dear Virgo, creativity flows easily. Whether you're working on a personal project, solving a problem, or exploring new ideas, today's energy supports innovation and outside-the-box thinking. Don't be afraid to experiment with different approaches or explore new possibilities. Your unique perspective will help you find exciting breakthroughs and fresh opportunities. Trust in your creative abilities, and let your imagination guide you toward success. Embrace the excitement of new ideas and creative expression.

Affirmation & Gratitude

"I embrace my creative spirit, allowing it to guide me toward new ideas and exciting possibilities."

 Virgo
29 August 2025

Today Dear Virgo, relationships are highlighted. Whether you're spending time with family, friends, or a romantic partner, today is a day to nurture your connections. Show appreciation for the people who bring joy to your life, and make an effort to strengthen your bonds. Meaningful conversations and thoughtful gestures will go a long way in deepening your relationships. Be present and attentive, and you'll find that your connections grow stronger and more fulfilling.

Affirmation & Gratitude

"I nurture my relationships with love and care, knowing that strong connections bring joy and fulfillment."

Virgo
30 August 2025

Today Dear Virgo, teamwork is emphasized. Whether you're working on a project at work, collaborating with friends, or spending time with family, today's energy supports cooperation and shared success. Be open to listening to others and offering your own insights. Together, you'll achieve more than you could alone. Trust in the power of collaboration and the value of community. Teamwork will lead to greater accomplishments and deeper connections. Celebrate the joy of working together toward common goals.

Affirmation & Gratitude

"I am grateful for the power of teamwork, knowing that collaboration leads to shared success and deeper connections."

Virgo
31 August 2025

Today Dear Virgo, your practical side shines. Today's energy supports organization, planning, and careful attention to detail. Whether you're managing a project or organizing your personal life, your logical thinking and practical nature will help you achieve success. Take the time to ensure that everything is in order, and don't rush through any tasks. Trust in your ability to plan and execute effectively, and your efforts will lead to positive outcomes. By the end of the day, you'll feel accomplished and satisfied with your progress.

Affirmation & Gratitude

"I trust my practical nature and attention to detail to guide me toward success and fulfillment."

September 2025

Virgo
01 September 2025

Today Dear Virgo, it's a great day to focus on self-improvement and personal growth. Reflect on your goals and the direction you're heading. Use this time to make adjustments where necessary and set new intentions. Whether through learning, self-reflection, or planning for the future, today's energy supports growth and transformation. Be open to evolving and improving in all areas of your life. By embracing change and progress, you'll find yourself moving closer to your aspirations.

Affirmation & Gratitude

"I embrace personal growth and trust in my ability to evolve and improve in all areas of my life."

Virgo
02 September 2025

Today Dear Virgo, relationships are in focus, and it's a great day to nurture your connections with loved ones. Whether through meaningful conversations, thoughtful gestures, or simply spending quality time, your efforts to strengthen your bonds will bring joy and harmony to your relationships. Be present and attentive with those you care about, and you'll find that love and understanding flow easily. Show appreciation for the important people in your life, and your relationships will grow even stronger.

Affirmation & Gratitude

"I nurture my relationships with love and care, knowing that strong connections bring joy and fulfillment."

Virgo
03 September 2025

Today Dear Virgo, creativity is at the forefront. Whether you're working on a personal project, solving problems, or exploring new ideas, today's energy supports thinking outside the box. Don't be afraid to experiment with different approaches or try something new. Your unique perspective will lead to exciting breakthroughs and fresh opportunities. Trust in your creative abilities, and let your imagination guide you toward success. Embrace the joy of creative expression and enjoy the freedom it brings.

Affirmation & Gratitude

"I embrace my creative spirit, allowing it to guide me toward new ideas and exciting possibilities."

Virgo
04 September 2025

Today Dear Virgo, communication is key. Whether you're resolving misunderstandings, having important conversations, or simply connecting with others, your ability to express yourself clearly and thoughtfully will lead to positive outcomes. Be open to listening to others and offering your insights with empathy. Today's energy supports healing and growth through dialogue, so don't hesitate to address unresolved issues. By fostering clear communication, you'll strengthen your relationships and build trust. Approach conversations with kindness and clarity.

Affirmation & Gratitude

"I communicate openly and kindly, trusting that clarity and understanding lead to stronger connections and healing."

Virgo

05 September 2025

Today Dear Virgo, balance is essential. You may feel pulled between work and personal obligations, but it's important to create harmony between the two. Focus on prioritizing your tasks and making time for relaxation. Don't spread yourself too thin—remember that balance is key to maintaining your well-being and staying productive. By creating structure and making time for self-care, you'll feel more centered and capable of handling the day's demands. Trust that balance will lead to peace and fulfillment.

Affirmation & Gratitude

"I create balance in my life, knowing that harmony between work and rest leads to peace and fulfillment."

Virgo

06 September 2025

Today Dear Virgo, your attention to detail will be your greatest asset. Whether you're working on a project, managing your tasks, or organizing your space, today's energy supports precision and careful planning. Take your time to ensure that everything is in order and don't rush through anything. Your practical nature and focus on the finer points will lead to success and a sense of accomplishment by the end of the day. Trust in your ability to navigate tasks with clarity and precision.

Affirmation & Gratitude

"I take pride in my attention to detail, knowing that it leads to excellence and success in all I do."

Virgo
07 September 2025

Today Dear Virgo, teamwork is emphasized. Whether you're collaborating on a project, working with colleagues, or engaging with loved ones, today's energy supports cooperation and shared success. Be open to listening to others and offering your insights. Together, you'll achieve more than you could alone. Trust in the power of collaboration, and embrace the support and contributions of those around you. Teamwork will lead to greater accomplishments and deeper connections.

Affirmation & Gratitude

"I am grateful for the power of teamwork, knowing that collaboration leads to shared success and deeper connections."

♍ Virgo
08 September 2025

Today Dear Virgo, creativity flows easily. Whether you're working on a personal project, solving a problem, or exploring new ideas, today's energy supports innovation and outside-the-box thinking. Don't be afraid to experiment with different approaches or explore new possibilities. Your unique perspective will help you find exciting breakthroughs and fresh opportunities. Trust in your creative abilities, and let your imagination guide you toward success. Embrace the excitement of new ideas and creative expression.

Affirmation & Gratitude

"I embrace my creative spirit, allowing it to guide me toward new ideas and exciting possibilities."

Virgo
09 September 2025

Today Dear Virgo, relationships take center stage. Whether you're connecting with family, friends, or a romantic partner, today's energy supports nurturing your bonds. Make an effort to show appreciation for the people who bring joy to your life. Meaningful conversations, acts of kindness, and quality time will deepen your connections and bring harmony to your relationships. Be present and attentive, and you'll find that love and understanding flow easily today.

Affirmation & Gratitude

"I nurture my relationships with love and care, knowing that strong connections bring joy and fulfillment."

Virgo
10 September 2025

Today Dear Virgo, communication is highlighted. Whether you're having important conversations, resolving a conflict, or simply connecting with others, your ability to express yourself clearly and thoughtfully will lead to positive results. Be open to hearing others' perspectives and offering your insights with empathy. Honest and open communication will build trust and strengthen your relationships. Don't hesitate to address any misunderstandings—today is a great day to foster understanding and connection through dialogue.

Affirmation & Gratitude

"I communicate openly and kindly, trusting that clarity and understanding lead to stronger connections and healing."

 Virgo
11 September 2025

Today Dear Virgo, balance is key. You may feel pulled between work and personal commitments, but it's important to create harmony in your day. Focus on prioritizing what's most important and make sure to take time for yourself. By maintaining balance, you'll feel more grounded and able to handle the day's demands with ease. Take care of your well-being as much as your responsibilities, and you'll find that balance brings peace and fulfillment.

Affirmation & Gratitude

"I create balance in my life, knowing that harmony between work and rest leads to peace and fulfillment."

Virgo
12 September 2025

Today Dear Virgo, your practical nature will shine. Whether you're organizing your space, managing your schedule, or tackling a big project, today's energy supports logical thinking and attention to detail. Take the time to approach tasks methodically and ensure that everything is in order. By staying focused and practical, you'll achieve positive results and feel a sense of accomplishment by the end of the day. Trust in your ability to organize and plan effectively.

Affirmation & Gratitude

"I trust my practical nature and attention to detail to guide me toward success and accomplishment."

Virgo
13 September 2025

Today Dear Virgo, self-care is essential. You've been busy lately, and today's energy encourages you to slow down and focus on your well-being. Whether through physical rest, emotional nourishment, or simply taking time to relax, prioritize your health and happiness today. By taking care of yourself, you'll restore your energy and feel more balanced. Don't underestimate the importance of self-care—it's a vital part of maintaining both productivity and peace of mind.

Affirmation & Gratitude

"I honor my body's need for rest and renewal, knowing that self-care is essential for my well-being."

Virgo

14 September 2025

Today Dear Virgo, your creativity is in full bloom. Whether you're working on a personal project, solving a problem, or exploring new ideas, today's energy supports thinking outside the box. Don't be afraid to experiment with different approaches or explore new possibilities. Your unique perspective will lead to exciting breakthroughs and new opportunities. Trust in your creative spirit, and let your imagination guide you toward success.

Affirmation & Gratitude

"I embrace my creative spirit, allowing it to guide me toward new ideas and exciting opportunities."

Virgo
15 September 2025

Today Dear Virgo, teamwork is emphasized. Whether you're collaborating on a project at work, working with friends, or spending time with family, today's energy supports cooperation and shared success. Be open to listening to others and offering your own insights. Together, you'll achieve greater results than you could alone. Trust in the power of teamwork, and celebrate the support and contributions of those around you. Collaboration will lead to mutual success and stronger connections.

Affirmation & Gratitude

"I am grateful for the power of teamwork, knowing that collaboration leads to shared success and deeper connections."

Virgo
16 September 2025

Today Dear Virgo, communication is key. Whether you're resolving a conflict, having important conversations, or simply connecting with others, your ability to express yourself clearly and thoughtfully will lead to positive outcomes. Be open to listening to others and offering your perspective with kindness. By fostering clear and respectful communication, you'll strengthen your relationships and build trust. Don't hesitate to address any misunderstandings—today is a great day for healing through dialogue.

Affirmation & Gratitude

"I communicate openly and honestly, trusting that clarity and understanding lead to stronger connections and healing."

Virgo
17 September 2025

Today Dear Virgo, balance is essential. You may feel pulled in different directions, but it's important to create harmony between work and personal life. Take the time to prioritize your tasks and ensure that you're giving equal attention to your well-being. By maintaining balance, you'll feel more grounded and ready to handle whatever comes your way. Make space for rest and relaxation, and you'll find that you're more productive and focused.

Affirmation & Gratitude

"I create balance in my life, knowing that harmony between work and rest leads to peace and fulfillment."

Virgo

18 September 2025

Today Dear Virgo, your analytical mind is your greatest asset today. Whether you're tackling a complex task, solving a problem, or organizing your day, your attention to detail will help you succeed. Take the time to think things through carefully and ensure that everything is in order. Your practical approach and methodical thinking will lead to positive results. Don't rush through anything—your careful planning will pay off. Trust in your analytical skills to guide you toward success.

Affirmation & Gratitude

"I trust my analytical mind to navigate challenges with clarity and focus, leading to success and fulfillment."

Virgo

19 September 2025

Today Dear Virgo, relationships are highlighted. Whether you're spending time with loved ones, reconnecting with friends, or deepening a romantic connection, today's energy supports love and harmony. Be present with those who matter most to you, and show appreciation for the joy and support they bring into your life. Thoughtful conversations and acts of kindness will strengthen your bonds and create lasting connections. Open your heart to love and understanding, and your relationships will flourish.

Affirmation & Gratitude

"I nurture my relationships with love and care, knowing that strong connections bring joy and fulfillment."

Virgo
20 September 2025

Today Dear Virgo, creativity flows easily. Whether you're working on a personal project, exploring new ideas, or solving a challenge, today's energy supports innovation and fresh perspectives. Don't hesitate to think outside the box and experiment with different approaches. Your creative abilities will lead to exciting breakthroughs and new opportunities. Trust in your creative spirit, and let your imagination guide you toward success. Embrace the excitement of new ideas and creative expression.

Affirmation & Gratitude

"I embrace my creative spirit, allowing it to guide me toward new ideas and exciting possibilities."

Virgo
21 September 2025

Today Dear Virgo, communication is key to success. Whether in your personal life or at work, your ability to express yourself clearly and thoughtfully will lead to positive results. Be open to listening to others and offering your perspective with empathy. Honest and open communication will build trust and strengthen your relationships. Don't shy away from important conversations—today's energy supports healing through dialogue. Approach every conversation with kindness and clarity, and you'll find understanding and resolution.

Affirmation & Gratitude

"I communicate openly and honestly, trusting that clarity and understanding lead to stronger connections and healing."

Virgo
22 September 2025

Today Dear Virgo, self-care is essential. You may feel the need to rest and recharge after a busy period. Take time to focus on your well-being, whether through physical rest, emotional nourishment, or simply taking time to slow down. Today's energy supports healing and renewal, so don't hesitate to take a break from your responsibilities. You'll return to your tasks feeling refreshed and ready to tackle what's ahead.

Affirmation & Gratitude

"I honor my body's need for rest and renewal, allowing myself to recharge and feel rejuvenated."

Virgo

23 September 2025

Today Dear Virgo, teamwork is emphasized. Whether you're collaborating on a project or working with friends and family, today's energy supports cooperation and shared success. Be open to others' ideas and contributions, and don't hesitate to offer your own insights. Working together will lead to greater achievements than you could accomplish alone. Trust in the power of collaboration and the value of community, and embrace the support that others offer.

Affirmation & Gratitude

"I am grateful for the power of teamwork, knowing that collaboration leads to shared success and deeper connections."

Virgo
24 September 2025

Today Dear Virgo, balance is important. You may feel pulled between work and personal commitments, but it's essential to create harmony in your day. Focus on prioritizing your tasks and make sure to take time for yourself. By maintaining balance, you'll feel more grounded and ready to handle the day's demands with ease. Take care of your well-being as much as your responsibilities, and you'll find that balance brings peace and fulfillment.

Affirmation & Gratitude

"I create balance in my life, knowing that harmony between work and rest leads to peace and fulfillment."

Virgo
25 September 2025

Today Dear Virgo, creativity is strong, and today's energy supports thinking outside the box. Whether you're working on a project, solving a problem, or exploring new ideas, allow your imagination to take the lead. Don't hesitate to try new approaches or experiment with different methods. Your creative abilities will help you discover new opportunities and breakthroughs. Trust in your ability to think innovatively, and you'll find success in unexpected ways. Embrace the excitement of creative expression.

Affirmation & Gratitude

"I embrace my creative spirit, allowing it to guide me toward new ideas and exciting possibilities."

♍ Virgo
26 September 2025

Today Dear Virgo, relationships are in focus. It's a great day to strengthen your bonds with loved ones, whether through thoughtful conversations, quality time, or acts of kindness. Be present and attentive with those who matter most, and you'll find that love and understanding flow easily today. Show appreciation for the people who bring joy to your life, and your relationships will deepen and grow stronger. Open your heart to love and connection, and you'll experience harmony in your interactions.

Affirmation & Gratitude

"I nurture my relationships with love and care, knowing that strong connections bring joy and fulfillment."

Virgo
27 September 2025

Today Dear Virgo, communication is highlighted. Whether you're resolving conflicts, having important conversations, or simply connecting with others, your ability to express yourself clearly and thoughtfully will lead to positive outcomes. Be open to listening to others and offering your perspective with kindness. By fostering honest and respectful communication, you'll strengthen your relationships and build trust. Don't hesitate to address any unresolved issues—today is a day for healing through dialogue.

Affirmation & Gratitude

"I communicate openly and kindly, trusting that clarity and understanding lead to stronger connections and healing."

Virgo
28 September 2025

Today Dear Virgo, your attention to detail will be a valuable asset today. Whether you're working on a project, organizing your space, or managing your tasks, your focus on precision will lead to success. Take your time to ensure that everything is done correctly, and don't rush through anything. Your practical nature and careful planning will lead to high-quality results and a sense of accomplishment by the end of the day. Trust in your ability to handle tasks with care and precision.

Affirmation & Gratitude

"I take pride in my attention to detail, knowing that it leads to excellence and success in all I do."

Virgo

29 September 2025

Today Dear Virgo, creativity is flowing. Whether you're working on a personal project, exploring new ideas, or finding innovative solutions to challenges, today's energy supports thinking outside the box. Don't be afraid to experiment with different approaches or try something new. Your unique perspective will lead to exciting breakthroughs and fresh opportunities. Trust in your creative abilities, and let your imagination guide you toward success. Embrace the freedom of creative expression and enjoy the possibilities that come with it.

Affirmation & Gratitude

"I embrace my creative spirit, allowing it to guide me toward new ideas and exciting opportunities."

Virgo

30 September 2025

Today Dear Virgo, balance is essential. You may feel pulled between work and personal obligations, but it's important to find harmony between the two. Focus on prioritizing your tasks and making time for relaxation. Don't spread yourself too thin—remember that balance is key to maintaining your well-being and staying productive. By creating structure and making time for self-care, you'll feel more centered and capable of handling the day's demands. Trust that balance will lead to peace and fulfillment.

Affirmation & Gratitude

"I create balance in my life, knowing that harmony between work and rest leads to peace and fulfillment."

October 2025

Virgo

01 October 2025

Today Dear Virgo, creativity is highlighted, making it an ideal day to explore new ideas and projects. Whether you're working on a personal goal or solving a problem, allow your imagination to guide you. Don't hesitate to try unconventional approaches or step outside your comfort zone. Fresh perspectives will lead to exciting breakthroughs. Trust in your ability to think innovatively, and let your creative spirit flourish. By embracing new possibilities, you'll discover solutions and opportunities that others may overlook.

Affirmation & Gratitude

"I embrace my creative spirit, allowing it to lead me toward new ideas and exciting possibilities."

Virgo
02 October 2025

Today Dear Virgo, balance is key. You may feel pulled in different directions by your responsibilities, but it's important to create harmony between work and personal time. Focus on prioritizing your tasks and make room for relaxation and self-care. By maintaining balance, you'll feel more centered and capable of handling everything on your plate. Remember that your well-being is as important as your productivity. A balanced approach will lead to peace and fulfillment.

Affirmation & Gratitude

"I create balance in my life, knowing that harmony between work and rest brings peace and fulfillment."

 Virgo
03 October 2025

Today Dear Virgo, relationships take center stage. Whether you're connecting with loved ones, spending time with family, or deepening friendships, today's energy supports nurturing your bonds. Be present and attentive in your interactions, and show appreciation for the important people in your life. Meaningful conversations and acts of kindness will strengthen your relationships, bringing joy and harmony. Trust that by nurturing your connections, you're building lasting and fulfilling relationships.

Affirmation & Gratitude

"I nurture my relationships with love and care, knowing that strong connections bring joy and fulfillment."

Virgo
04 October 2025

Today Dear Virgo, your analytical mind is in full force, making it a great day to focus on problem-solving and tasks that require attention to detail. Whether at work or home, you'll find satisfaction in breaking down complex issues and finding practical solutions. Don't rush through your tasks—take your time to think things through carefully. Your methodical approach will ensure that you achieve the best possible outcomes. Trust in your ability to tackle any challenges that arise today with clarity and precision.

Affirmation & Gratitude

"I trust my analytical mind to navigate challenges with clarity and precision, leading to success and fulfillment."

Virgo
05 October 2025

Today Dear Virgo, communication is key. Whether you're resolving conflicts, having important conversations, or simply connecting with others, your ability to express yourself clearly and thoughtfully will lead to positive outcomes. Be open to listening to others and offering your perspective with kindness. By fostering open and honest communication, you'll strengthen your relationships and build trust. Don't hesitate to address any misunderstandings—today's energy supports healing through dialogue. Approach conversations with empathy and clarity.

Affirmation & Gratitude

"I communicate openly and kindly, trusting that clarity and understanding lead to stronger and healthier connections."

Virgo
06 October 2025

Today Dear Virgo, balance is essential. You may feel pulled between work and personal obligations, but it's important to find harmony between the two. Focus on prioritizing your tasks and make sure to take time for yourself. By maintaining balance, you'll feel more grounded and ready to handle the day's demands with ease. Take care of your well-being as much as your responsibilities, and you'll find that balance brings peace and fulfillment.

Affirmation & Gratitude

"I create balance in my life, knowing that harmony between work and rest leads to peace and fulfillment."

Virgo

07 October 2025

Today Dear Virgo, your practical nature shines through as you focus on organization and planning. Whether you're managing a project or tidying up your personal life, today's energy supports logical thinking and attention to detail. Take the time to create a clear plan for your tasks, and don't rush through anything. Your ability to organize and prioritize will lead to success and a sense of accomplishment. Trust in your practical skills to guide you toward positive outcomes.

Affirmation & Gratitude

"I trust my practical nature and attention to detail to guide me toward success and accomplishment."

Virgo
08 October 2025

Today Dear Virgo, creativity flows easily, making it a perfect day to work on personal projects or explore new ideas. Whether you're tackling a creative challenge or simply finding new solutions, today's energy supports innovation and outside-the-box thinking. Don't hesitate to experiment with different approaches—your imagination will lead to exciting breakthroughs and fresh opportunities. Trust in your creative abilities and allow your curiosity to guide you toward success. Embrace the freedom of creative expression and the possibilities it brings.

Affirmation & Gratitude

"I embrace my creative spirit, allowing it to guide me toward new ideas and exciting possibilities."

Virgo
09 October 2025

Today Dear Virgo, relationships are highlighted. Whether you're spending time with family, friends, or a romantic partner, today is a day to nurture your connections. Show appreciation for the people who bring joy to your life, and make an effort to strengthen your bonds. Meaningful conversations and thoughtful gestures will go a long way in deepening your relationships. Be present and attentive, and you'll find that your connections grow stronger and more fulfilling.

Affirmation & Gratitude

"I nurture my relationships with love and care, knowing that strong connections bring joy and fulfillment."

 Virgo
10 October 2025

Today Dear Virgo, balance is key to staying grounded. You may have a lot on your plate, but it's important to create harmony between work and personal obligations. Prioritize your tasks and make sure to take time for yourself. By maintaining balance, you'll feel more centered and ready to tackle your responsibilities with ease. Don't overlook the importance of self-care—creating a balanced routine will lead to peace and productivity.

Affirmation & Gratitude

"I create balance in my life, knowing that harmony between work and rest leads to peace and fulfillment."

 Virgo
11 October 2025

Today Dear Virgo, your analytical nature will help you navigate complex tasks. Whether you're solving a problem, managing your workload, or organizing your personal life, today's energy supports logical thinking and careful planning. Take your time to ensure that everything is done correctly, and don't rush through anything. Your attention to detail will lead to success and a sense of accomplishment. Trust in your problem-solving abilities and your methodical approach.

Affirmation & Gratitude

"I trust my analytical mind to approach challenges with clarity and precision, leading to success and satisfaction."

Virgo
12 October 2025

Today Dear Virgo, communication is key to success. Whether in your personal life or at work, your ability to express yourself clearly and thoughtfully will lead to positive results. Be open to listening to others and offer your perspective with empathy. Honest and open communication will build trust and strengthen your relationships. Don't shy away from important conversations—today's energy supports healing through dialogue. Approach every conversation with kindness and clarity, and you'll find understanding and resolution.

Affirmation & Gratitude

"I communicate openly and kindly, trusting that clarity and understanding lead to stronger connections and healing."

 Virgo
13 October 2025

Today Dear Virgo, creativity is your ally. Whether you're working on a personal project, brainstorming ideas, or tackling a challenge, today's energy supports thinking outside the box. Don't be afraid to try new approaches and experiment with different methods. Your innovative thinking will lead to breakthroughs and fresh solutions that others might overlook. Trust in your ability to see things from a unique perspective, and let your creativity guide you toward success.

Affirmation & Gratitude

"I embrace my creative spirit, allowing it to guide me toward new ideas and exciting possibilities."

Virgo
14 October 2025

Today Dear Virgo, relationships take center stage. Whether you're spending time with loved ones, reconnecting with friends, or deepening a romantic connection, today's energy supports love and harmony. Be present and attentive with those who matter most to you, and show appreciation for the joy and support they bring into your life. Thoughtful conversations and acts of kindness will strengthen your bonds and create lasting connections. Open your heart to love and understanding, and your relationships will flourish.

Affirmation & Gratitude

"I nurture my relationships with love and care, knowing that strong connections bring joy and fulfillment."

 Virgo

15 October 2025

Today Dear Virgo, your creative energy is strong. Whether you're working on a personal project, exploring new ideas, or finding innovative solutions to challenges, today's energy supports thinking outside the box. Don't hesitate to experiment with different approaches or try something new. Your unique perspective will lead to exciting breakthroughs and fresh opportunities. Trust in your creative abilities, and let your imagination guide you toward success. Embrace the freedom of creative expression.

Affirmation & Gratitude

"I embrace my creative spirit, allowing it to guide me toward new ideas and exciting opportunities."

Virgo
16 October 2025

Today Dear Virgo, balance is important. You may feel pulled between work and personal obligations, but it's essential to create harmony between the two. Focus on prioritizing your tasks and make sure to take time for yourself. By maintaining balance, you'll feel more grounded and ready to handle the day's demands with ease. Take care of your well-being as much as your responsibilities, and you'll find that balance brings peace and fulfillment.

Affirmation & Gratitude

"I create balance in my life, knowing that harmony between work and rest leads to peace and fulfillment."

Virgo
17 October 2025

Today Dear Virgo, communication is highlighted. Whether you're having important conversations, resolving a conflict, or simply connecting with others, your ability to express yourself clearly and thoughtfully will lead to positive outcomes. Be open to hearing others' perspectives and offering your insights with empathy. Honest and open communication will build trust and strengthen your relationships. Don't hesitate to address any misunderstandings—today is a great day to foster understanding and connection through dialogue.

Affirmation & Gratitude

"I communicate openly and kindly, trusting that clarity and understanding lead to stronger connections and healing."

Virgo
18 October 2025

Today Dear Virgo, self-care is essential. You may feel the need to rest and recharge after a busy period. Take time to focus on your well-being, whether through physical rest, emotional nourishment, or simply taking time to slow down. Today's energy supports healing and renewal, so don't hesitate to take a break from your responsibilities. You'll return to your tasks feeling refreshed and ready to tackle what's ahead.

Affirmation & Gratitude

"I honor my body's need for rest and renewal, allowing myself to recharge and feel rejuvenated."

Virgo
19 October 2025

Today Dear Virgo, teamwork is emphasized. Whether you're collaborating on a project or working with friends and family, today's energy supports cooperation and shared success. Be open to others' ideas and contributions, and don't hesitate to offer your own insights. Working together will lead to greater achievements than you could accomplish alone. Trust in the power of collaboration and the value of community, and embrace the support that others offer.

Affirmation & Gratitude

"I am grateful for the power of teamwork, knowing that collaboration leads to shared success and deeper connections."

Virgo
20 October 2025

Today Dear Virgo, balance is key. Whether you're juggling work responsibilities or personal commitments, today's energy encourages you to create harmony in your day. Focus on prioritizing what's most important, but don't forget to take time for self-care and relaxation. By finding balance, you'll feel more centered and capable of handling everything on your plate. Trust that balance will lead to both productivity and peace.

Affirmation & Gratitude

"I create balance in my life, knowing that harmony between work and rest leads to peace and fulfillment."

# Virgo
21 October 2025

Today Dear Virgo, your focus is on relationships. Whether you're spending time with loved ones, reconnecting with friends, or nurturing a romantic connection, today is a day to strengthen your bonds. Be present and attentive with those who matter most to you, and show appreciation for the joy and support they bring into your life. Meaningful conversations and thoughtful gestures will deepen your relationships and create lasting connections. Open your heart to love and connection.

Affirmation & Gratitude

"I nurture my relationships with love and care, knowing that strong connections bring joy and fulfillment."

Virgo
22 October 2025

Today Dear Virgo, creativity flows easily. Whether you're working on a personal project, exploring new ideas, or solving a problem, today's energy supports innovation and outside-the-box thinking. Don't be afraid to experiment with different approaches or explore new possibilities. Your unique perspective will help you find exciting breakthroughs and fresh opportunities. Trust in your creative abilities, and let your imagination guide you toward success. Embrace the excitement of new ideas and creative expression.

Affirmation & Gratitude

"I embrace my creative spirit, allowing it to guide me toward new ideas and exciting possibilities."

Virgo
23 October 2025

Today Dear Virgo, communication is key. Whether you're resolving misunderstandings, having important conversations, or simply connecting with others, your ability to express yourself clearly and thoughtfully will lead to positive outcomes. Be open to hearing others' perspectives and offering your insights with empathy. Today's energy supports healing and growth through dialogue, so don't hesitate to address unresolved issues. By fostering clear communication, you'll strengthen your relationships and build trust.

Affirmation & Gratitude

"I communicate openly and kindly, trusting that clarity and understanding lead to stronger connections and healing."

Virgo
24 October 2025

Today Dear Virgo, balance is essential. You may feel pulled between responsibilities, but it's important to create harmony between work and personal life. Focus on prioritizing your tasks and make time for self-care and relaxation. By maintaining balance, you'll feel more grounded and capable of handling the day's challenges with ease. Don't overlook the importance of caring for yourself alongside your responsibilities. A balanced approach will lead to peace and productivity.

Affirmation & Gratitude

"I create balance in my life, knowing that harmony between work and rest leads to peace and fulfillment."

Virgo
25 October 2025

Today Dear Virgo, your creative energy is in full swing. Whether you're working on a personal project, solving problems, or exploring new ideas, today's energy supports thinking outside the box. Don't hesitate to try new approaches or experiment with different methods. Your innovative thinking will lead to breakthroughs and exciting opportunities. Trust in your creative spirit, and let it guide you toward success. Embrace the excitement that comes from creative exploration.

Affirmation & Gratitude

"I embrace my creative spirit, allowing it to guide me toward new ideas and exciting opportunities."

Virgo
26 October 2025

Today Dear Virgo, relationships are highlighted. Whether you're spending time with family, friends, or a romantic partner, today's energy supports nurturing your connections. Show appreciation for the people who bring joy and support into your life, and make an effort to strengthen your bonds. Meaningful conversations and acts of kindness will go a long way in deepening your relationships. Be present and attentive, and you'll find that love and understanding flow easily.

Affirmation & Gratitude

"I nurture my relationships with love and care, knowing that strong connections bring joy and fulfillment."

 Virgo
27 October 2025

Today Dear Virgo, balance is key. Whether you're managing work responsibilities or personal commitments, it's important to create harmony in your day. Focus on what's most important, but don't forget to take time for yourself. By finding balance, you'll feel more grounded and able to handle your tasks with ease. Don't overextend yourself—remember that maintaining your well-being is just as important as fulfilling your obligations.

Affirmation & Gratitude

"I create balance in my life, knowing that harmony between work and rest leads to peace and fulfillment."

Virgo
28 October 2025

Today Dear Virgo, teamwork is emphasized. Whether you're collaborating on a project at work, working with friends, or spending time with family, today's energy supports cooperation and shared success. Be open to listening to others and offering your own insights. Together, you'll achieve greater results than you could alone. Trust in the power of collaboration and embrace the support of those around you. Teamwork will lead to mutual success and deeper connections.

Affirmation & Gratitude

"I am grateful for the power of teamwork, knowing that collaboration leads to shared success and deeper connections."

Virgo
29 October 2025

Today Dear Virgo, communication is key. Whether you're having important conversations, resolving a conflict, or simply connecting with others, your ability to express yourself clearly and thoughtfully will lead to positive outcomes. Be open to listening to others and offering your insights with empathy. Honest and open communication will build trust and strengthen your relationships. Don't hesitate to address any misunderstandings—today is a great day for healing through dialogue.

Affirmation & Gratitude

"I communicate openly and kindly, trusting that clarity and understanding lead to stronger connections and healing."

Virgo
30 October 2025

Today Dear Virgo, your practical nature is in high demand. Whether you're managing a project, organizing your home, or planning for the future, today's energy supports logical thinking and attention to detail. Take the time to carefully plan and prioritize your tasks, and don't rush through anything. Your ability to stay organized and focused will lead to success and a sense of accomplishment. Trust in your practical approach to guide you toward positive outcomes, and take pride in your efforts today.

Affirmation & Gratitude

"I trust my practical nature and attention to detail to guide me toward success and fulfillment."

 Virgo
31 October 2025

Today Dear Virgo, creativity is at the forefront. Whether you're working on a personal project, solving problems, or exploring new ideas, today's energy supports thinking outside the box. Don't hesitate to experiment with new approaches or explore new possibilities. Your unique perspective will help you discover exciting breakthroughs and opportunities that others might miss. Trust in your creative spirit and let it lead you toward innovative solutions and fresh ideas.

Affirmation & Gratitude

"I embrace my creative spirit, allowing it to guide me toward new ideas and exciting possibilities."

November 2025

Virgo
01 November 2025

Today Dear Virgo, it's a day for reflection and self-improvement. Take time to assess where you are in your personal journey. Focus on growth and self-awareness. Today's energy encourages you to set new goals or realign with your current ones. Embrace any changes that feel necessary for your overall well-being. Self-reflection will help you gain clarity on the path ahead, and you'll feel more prepared for future challenges. Trust in your ability to evolve and improve with each step forward.

Affirmation & Gratitude

"I embrace self-reflection and personal growth, trusting that each step brings me closer to my goals and fulfillment."

Virgo
02 November 2025

Today Dear Virgo, creativity is in full flow. Whether you're working on a project, problem-solving, or exploring new ideas, today's energy encourages innovative thinking. Don't be afraid to try different approaches or think outside the box. Your imagination will lead you to exciting possibilities and breakthroughs. Trust your creative abilities and follow your instincts. Embrace the freedom that comes with creative expression, and enjoy the process of discovery. Your fresh perspectives will open up new doors of opportunity.

Affirmation & Gratitude

"I embrace my creative spirit, allowing it to lead me toward new ideas and exciting possibilities."

Virgo

03 November 2025

Today Dear Virgo, balance is key. You may be feeling the pressure of work and personal commitments, but it's important to create harmony between both. Prioritize your tasks and make sure to carve out time for relaxation. By maintaining balance, you'll feel more grounded and capable of managing your responsibilities. Don't let stress overwhelm you—taking care of your well-being is essential for long-term productivity. Trust that balance leads to peace and fulfillment, and make time for self-care today.

Affirmation & Gratitude

"I create balance in my life, knowing that harmony between work and rest leads to peace and fulfillment."

Virgo

04 November 2025

Today Dear Virgo, relationships are highlighted. Whether you're spending time with loved ones, reconnecting with friends, or nurturing a romantic bond, today's energy supports deepening your connections. Be present and attentive in your interactions, and show appreciation for the people who bring joy and support to your life. Thoughtful conversations and small acts of kindness will go a long way in strengthening your relationships. Don't be afraid to express your feelings and build stronger emotional bonds with those who matter most.

Affirmation & Gratitude

"I nurture my relationships with love and care, knowing that strong connections bring joy and fulfillment."

 Virgo
05 November 2025

Today Dear Virgo, communication is essential. Whether you're resolving a misunderstanding, having an important conversation, or simply connecting with others, your ability to express yourself clearly and thoughtfully will lead to positive outcomes. Be open to listening and sharing your perspective with kindness. Honest dialogue will strengthen your relationships and build trust. Today's energy supports healing through open communication, so don't hesitate to address any unresolved issues. Approach conversations with empathy and clarity, and you'll foster understanding and resolution.

Affirmation & Gratitude

"I communicate openly and kindly, trusting that clarity and understanding lead to stronger connections and healing."

Virgo

06 November 2025

Today Dear Virgo, self-care is essential. You've been pushing yourself hard lately, and today's energy encourages you to take a break and focus on your well-being. Whether through physical rest, emotional healing, or mental relaxation, prioritize your health today. By recharging, you'll restore your energy and be better prepared to handle the demands of life. Don't feel guilty for resting—self-care is a necessary part of staying balanced and productive. Take time to nurture yourself, and you'll feel renewed.

Affirmation & Gratitude

"I honor my body's need for rest and renewal, knowing that self-care is essential for my well-being."

Virgo
07 November 2025

Today Dear Virgo, your practical side will shine. Whether you're managing a project, organizing your space, or planning for the future, today's energy supports logical thinking and attention to detail. Take the time to plan out your day or week, and don't rush through any tasks. Your ability to stay organized and focused will lead to success and a sense of accomplishment. Trust in your practical approach, and let it guide you toward positive outcomes. By the end of the day, you'll feel a sense of achievement.

Affirmation & Gratitude

"I trust my practical nature and attention to detail to guide me toward success and fulfillment."

Virgo

08 November 2025

Today Dear Virgo, creativity is flowing, and it's a great day to work on personal projects or explore new ideas. Today's energy supports thinking outside the box and trying new approaches. Don't be afraid to experiment and embrace innovative ideas—your imagination will lead you to exciting breakthroughs and opportunities. Whether it's a creative challenge or finding fresh solutions, trust in your ability to bring new ideas to life. Embrace the joy of creative expression, and allow yourself to dream big.

Affirmation & Gratitude

"I embrace my creative spirit, allowing it to guide me toward new ideas and exciting possibilities."

Virgo
09 November 2025

Today Dear Virgo, relationships take center stage. Whether you're spending time with loved ones, connecting with friends, or strengthening a romantic bond, today's energy supports love and harmony. Be present and engaged with the people who matter most to you, and show appreciation for the joy they bring into your life. Thoughtful gestures and meaningful conversations will deepen your connections and create a stronger sense of togetherness. Open your heart to love and understanding, and you'll find that your relationships grow even stronger.

Affirmation & Gratitude

"I nurture my relationships with love and care, knowing that strong connections bring joy and fulfillment."

Virgo
10 November 2025

Today Dear Virgo, communication is highlighted. Whether you're resolving conflicts, having important discussions, or simply connecting with others, your ability to express yourself clearly and thoughtfully will lead to positive results. Be open to listening and offering your perspective with kindness. Honest and open communication will build trust and strengthen your relationships. Don't hesitate to address any misunderstandings—today is a day for healing through dialogue. Approach every conversation with empathy and clarity, and you'll find understanding and resolution.

Affirmation & Gratitude

"I communicate openly and kindly, trusting that clarity and understanding lead to stronger connections and healing."

Virgo
11 November 2025

Today Dear Virgo, your analytical mind is your greatest asset today. Whether you're tackling complex tasks, solving a problem, or organizing your day, your attention to detail will help you succeed. Take the time to think things through carefully and ensure that everything is in order. Your practical approach and methodical thinking will lead to positive results. Don't rush through anything—your careful planning will pay off. Trust in your analytical skills to guide you toward success and fulfillment.

Affirmation & Gratitude

"I trust my analytical mind to navigate challenges with clarity and focus, leading to success and satisfaction."

Virgo
12 November 2025

Today Dear Virgo, balance is key. Whether you're juggling work responsibilities or personal obligations, today's energy encourages you to find harmony in your day. Focus on prioritizing what's most important, but don't forget to take time for self-care and relaxation. By maintaining balance, you'll feel more grounded and able to handle everything that comes your way. Take care of your well-being as much as your responsibilities, and you'll find that balance brings peace and fulfillment.

Affirmation & Gratitude

"I create balance in my life, knowing that harmony between work and rest leads to peace and fulfillment."

Virgo

13 November 2025

Today Dear Virgo, teamwork is emphasized. Whether you're collaborating on a project at work or spending time with friends and family, today's energy supports cooperation and shared success. Be open to listening to others and offering your insights. Together, you'll achieve more than you could alone. Trust in the power of collaboration, and embrace the support of those around you. Teamwork will lead to greater accomplishments and deeper connections. Celebrate the joy of working together toward common goals.

Affirmation & Gratitude

"I am grateful for the power of teamwork, knowing that collaboration leads to shared success and deeper connections."

Virgo

14 November 2025

Today Dear Virgo, creativity is your ally. Whether you're working on a personal project, brainstorming ideas, or tackling a challenge, today's energy supports thinking outside the box. Don't be afraid to try new approaches and experiment with different methods. Your innovative thinking will lead to breakthroughs and fresh solutions that others might overlook. Trust in your ability to see things from a unique perspective, and let your creativity guide you toward success.

Affirmation & Gratitude

"I embrace my creative spirit, allowing it to guide me toward new ideas and exciting possibilities."

Virgo
15 November 2025

Today Dear Virgo, relationships are in focus, and today is a great day to nurture your connections with loved ones. Whether through meaningful conversations, thoughtful gestures, or simply spending quality time, your efforts to strengthen your bonds will be rewarded. Be present and attentive in your interactions, and show appreciation for the people who bring joy to your life. Love and understanding will flow easily today, deepening your bonds and creating harmony in your relationships.

Affirmation & Gratitude

"I nurture my relationships with love and care, knowing that strong connections bring joy and fulfillment."

Virgo
16 November 2025

Today Dear Virgo, balance is essential. You may feel pulled between work and personal obligations, but it's important to create harmony between the two. Focus on prioritizing your tasks and make room for relaxation. Don't spread yourself too thin—remember that balance is key to maintaining your well-being and staying productive. By creating structure and making time for self-care, you'll feel more centered and capable of handling the day's demands. Trust that balance will lead to peace and fulfillment.

Affirmation & Gratitude

"I create balance in my life, knowing that harmony between work and rest leads to peace and fulfillment."

Virgo

17 November 2025

Today Dear Virgo, communication is key. Whether you're resolving a conflict, having important conversations, or simply connecting with others, your ability to express yourself clearly and thoughtfully will lead to positive outcomes. Be open to listening to others and offering your perspective with empathy. Honest and open communication will build trust and strengthen your relationships. Don't hesitate to address any unresolved issues—today is a great day for healing through dialogue.

Affirmation & Gratitude

"I communicate openly and kindly, trusting that clarity and understanding lead to stronger connections and healing."

Virgo
18 November 2025

Today Dear Virgo, creativity is flowing, and it's a great day to work on personal projects or explore new ideas. Today's energy supports thinking outside the box and trying new approaches. Don't be afraid to experiment and embrace innovative ideas—your imagination will lead you to exciting breakthroughs and opportunities. Whether it's a creative challenge or finding fresh solutions, trust in your ability to bring new ideas to life. Embrace the joy of creative expression, and allow yourself to dream big.

Affirmation & Gratitude

"I embrace my creative spirit, allowing it to guide me toward new ideas and exciting possibilities."

Virgo
19 November 2025

Today Dear Virgo, teamwork is emphasized. Whether you're working with colleagues on a project, collaborating with friends, or spending time with family, today's energy supports cooperation and shared success. Be open to others' ideas and contributions, and don't hesitate to offer your own insights. By working together, you'll accomplish more than you could alone. Trust in the value of collaboration, and appreciate the support and input of those around you. Teamwork will lead to greater accomplishments and deeper connections.

Affirmation & Gratitude

"I am grateful for the power of teamwork, knowing that collaboration leads to shared success and deeper connections."

Virgo
20 November 2025

Today Dear Virgo, your practical side shines today. Whether you're organizing your space, managing a project, or planning for the future, today's energy supports logical thinking and attention to detail. Take the time to plan out your day and ensure that everything is in order. Your practical approach will lead to success and a sense of accomplishment by the end of the day. Trust in your ability to navigate challenges with clarity and precision. By staying organized and focused, you'll feel confident in your progress.

Affirmation & Gratitude

"I trust my practical nature and attention to detail to guide me toward success and fulfillment."

 Virgo

21 November 2025

Today Dear Virgo, balance is important. Whether you're managing work responsibilities or personal commitments, today's energy encourages you to create harmony in your day. Focus on prioritizing what's most important, but don't forget to take time for self-care and relaxation. By maintaining balance, you'll feel more grounded and able to handle everything on your plate. Trust that balance will lead to both productivity and peace.

Affirmation & Gratitude

"I create balance in my life, knowing that harmony between work and rest leads to peace and fulfillment."

Virgo
22 November 2025

Today Dear Virgo, relationships take center stage. Whether you're connecting with loved ones, deepening friendships, or nurturing a romantic bond, today's energy supports love and harmony. Be present and attentive with those who matter most, and show appreciation for the joy and support they bring into your life. Meaningful conversations and thoughtful gestures will deepen your connections and create lasting bonds. Open your heart to love and understanding, and your relationships will flourish.

Affirmation & Gratitude

"I nurture my relationships with love and care, knowing that strong connections bring joy and fulfillment."

Virgo

23 November 2025

Today Dear Virgo, creativity is highlighted. Whether you're working on a personal project, solving a problem, or exploring new ideas, today's energy supports thinking outside the box. Don't hesitate to try new approaches or experiment with different methods. Your unique perspective will help you discover exciting breakthroughs and fresh opportunities. Trust in your creative spirit, and let your imagination guide you toward success. Embrace the excitement of new ideas and creative expression.

Affirmation & Gratitude

"I embrace my creative spirit, allowing it to guide me toward new ideas and exciting possibilities."

Virgo
24 November 2025

Today Dear Virgo, communication is essential. Whether you're resolving a conflict, having an important conversation, or simply connecting with others, your ability to express yourself clearly and thoughtfully will lead to positive outcomes. Be open to listening and offering your perspective with kindness. By fostering open and honest communication, you'll strengthen your relationships and build trust. Don't hesitate to address any unresolved issues—today's energy supports healing through dialogue.

Affirmation & Gratitude

"I communicate openly and kindly, trusting that clarity and understanding lead to stronger connections and healing."

Virgo

25 November 2025

Today Dear Virgo, balance is essential. You may feel pulled in different directions by your responsibilities, but it's important to create harmony between work and personal obligations. Prioritize your tasks and make sure to carve out time for relaxation. By maintaining balance, you'll feel more centered and capable of handling everything on your plate. Remember that your well-being is as important as your productivity. A balanced approach will lead to peace and fulfillment.

Affirmation & Gratitude

"I create balance in my life, knowing that harmony between work and rest brings peace and fulfillment."

Virgo
26 November 2025

Today Dear Virgo, self-care is important. You've been working hard, and today's energy encourages you to take time for yourself. Whether through rest, relaxation, or emotional nourishment, prioritize your well-being today. By focusing on self-care, you'll recharge your energy and feel more balanced. Don't underestimate the importance of taking care of yourself—it's a vital part of maintaining long-term health and happiness. Treat yourself with kindness and compassion, and you'll return to your responsibilities feeling refreshed and ready.

Affirmation & Gratitude

"I honor my body's need for rest and renewal, knowing that self-care is essential for my well-being."

Virgo

27 November 2025

Today Dear Virgo, creativity flows easily. Whether you're working on a personal project, exploring new ideas, or solving a challenge, today's energy supports innovative thinking. Don't hesitate to think outside the box and try new approaches. Your unique perspective will lead to exciting breakthroughs and fresh opportunities. Trust in your creative abilities, and let your imagination guide you toward success. Embrace the freedom of creative expression, and enjoy the possibilities that come with it.

Affirmation & Gratitude

"I embrace my creative spirit, allowing it to guide me toward new ideas and exciting possibilities."

Virgo

28 November 2025

Today Dear Virgo, balance is key. You may feel pulled between work responsibilities and personal obligations, but it's important to find harmony between the two. Focus on prioritizing your tasks and make sure to take time for self-care. By maintaining balance, you'll feel more centered and ready to handle the demands of the day. Remember that balance is essential for both productivity and well-being. Make time for rest and relaxation, and you'll find that everything falls into place.

Affirmation & Gratitude

"I create balance in my life, knowing that harmony between work and rest leads to peace and fulfillment."

Virgo
29 November 2025

Today Dear Virgo, communication is highlighted. Whether you're resolving misunderstandings, having important conversations, or simply connecting with others, your ability to express yourself clearly and thoughtfully will lead to positive outcomes. Be open to hearing others' perspectives and offering your insights with empathy. Today's energy supports healing and growth through dialogue, so don't hesitate to address unresolved issues. By fostering clear communication, you'll strengthen your relationships and build trust. Approach conversations with kindness and clarity.

Affirmation & Gratitude

"I communicate openly and kindly, trusting that clarity and understanding lead to stronger connections and healing."

Virgo

30 November 2025

Today Dear Virgo, creativity is in full bloom. Whether you're working on a project, solving problems, or exploring new ideas, today's energy supports thinking outside the box. Don't hesitate to experiment with new approaches or explore new possibilities. Your unique perspective will help you discover exciting breakthroughs and opportunities that others might miss. Trust in your creative spirit, and let it lead you toward innovative solutions and fresh ideas. Embrace the freedom of creative expression.

Affirmation & Gratitude

"I embrace my creative spirit, allowing it to guide me toward new ideas and exciting possibilities."

December 2025

Virgo
01 December 2025

Today Dear Virgo, it's a day for self-reflection and goal-setting. As the year begins to close, take time to assess your progress and think about what you want to achieve moving forward. Today's energy encourages you to set clear intentions for the upcoming year. Whether it's personal growth, professional goals, or emotional healing, trust that you're capable of making the changes necessary for success. Take small steps toward your vision, and trust in your ability to manifest your desires.

Affirmation & Gratitude

"I reflect on my progress and set clear intentions, trusting in my ability to achieve my goals."

Virgo
02 December 2025

Today Dear Virgo, creativity is flowing. Whether you're working on a personal project, brainstorming ideas, or tackling a problem, today's energy supports innovative thinking. Don't be afraid to experiment with new approaches or think outside the box. Your unique perspective will help you uncover fresh solutions and exciting opportunities. Trust in your creative instincts and allow your imagination to lead the way. Embrace the joy of creative expression and explore the possibilities that come with it.

Affirmation & Gratitude

"I embrace my creative spirit, allowing it to lead me toward new ideas and exciting possibilities."

Virgo
03 December 2025

Today Dear Virgo, relationships are highlighted, and it's a great day to strengthen your connections with loved ones. Whether through thoughtful gestures, meaningful conversations, or quality time, your efforts will deepen your relationships. Show appreciation for the important people in your life and be fully present with them today. Love and understanding will flow easily, bringing joy and harmony to your relationships. By nurturing your connections, you'll create lasting bonds that bring fulfillment and happiness.

Affirmation & Gratitude

"I nurture my relationships with love and care, knowing that strong connections bring joy and fulfillment."

Virgo

04 December 2025

Today Dear Virgo, balance is key. You may feel pulled between work and personal obligations, but it's important to find harmony between the two. Focus on prioritizing your tasks and ensure that you're giving yourself the time and space for self-care. By maintaining balance, you'll feel more grounded and able to manage your responsibilities with ease. Remember that your well-being is just as important as your productivity. Take care of yourself, and everything else will fall into place.

Affirmation & Gratitude

"I create balance in my life, knowing that harmony between work and rest leads to peace and fulfillment."

Virgo
05 December 2025

Today Dear Virgo, your practical nature shines through as you focus on organization and planning. Whether you're managing your tasks or preparing for future projects, today's energy supports logical thinking and attention to detail. Take time to carefully plan and prioritize, ensuring that everything is in order. Your ability to stay organized and methodical will lead to success and a sense of accomplishment. Trust in your practical skills to guide you toward positive outcomes.

Affirmation & Gratitude

"I trust my practical nature and attention to detail to guide me toward success and accomplishment."

Virgo
06 December 2025

Today Dear Virgo, communication is key. Whether you're having important conversations, resolving conflicts, or simply connecting with others, your ability to express yourself clearly and thoughtfully will lead to positive results. Be open to listening to others and offering your perspective with kindness. Honest and open dialogue will strengthen your relationships and build trust. Don't hesitate to address any unresolved issues—today's energy supports healing through communication. Approach every conversation with empathy and clarity.

Affirmation & Gratitude

"I communicate openly and kindly, trusting that clarity and understanding lead to stronger connections and healing."

Virgo

07 December 2025

Today Dear Virgo, creativity is in full swing, and today's energy supports thinking outside the box. Whether you're working on a creative project, solving a problem, or exploring new ideas, let your imagination run free. Don't be afraid to try new approaches or experiment with fresh ideas. Your unique perspective will lead to exciting breakthroughs and opportunities. Trust in your creative abilities and allow yourself to embrace the joy of discovery.

Affirmation & Gratitude

"I embrace my creative spirit, allowing it to guide me toward new ideas and exciting possibilities."

Virgo
08 December 2025

Today Dear Virgo, teamwork is emphasized. Whether you're collaborating on a project at work or spending time with family and friends, today's energy supports cooperation and shared success. Be open to others' ideas and contributions, and don't hesitate to offer your insights. Working together will lead to greater achievements than you could accomplish alone. Trust in the value of collaboration and appreciate the support of those around you. Teamwork will lead to mutual success and deeper connections.

Affirmation & Gratitude

"I am grateful for the power of teamwork, knowing that collaboration leads to shared success and deeper connections."

 Virgo
09 December 2025

Today Dear Virgo, relationships are in focus. Whether you're spending time with loved ones, reconnecting with friends, or deepening a romantic connection, today's energy supports nurturing your bonds. Be present with those who matter most and show appreciation for the joy they bring to your life. Thoughtful gestures and meaningful conversations will deepen your relationships and create lasting connections. Open your heart to love and understanding, and your relationships will flourish.

Affirmation & Gratitude

"I nurture my relationships with love and care, knowing that strong connections bring joy and fulfillment."

Virgo
10 December 2025

Today Dear Virgo, balance is key. You may feel pulled in different directions, but it's important to find harmony between work and personal life. Focus on prioritizing your tasks and make sure to take time for relaxation and self-care. By maintaining balance, you'll feel more centered and ready to handle the day's challenges. Trust that balance will lead to both productivity and peace. Take care of yourself, and you'll find that everything else falls into place naturally.

Affirmation & Gratitude

"I create balance in my life, knowing that harmony between work and rest leads to peace and fulfillment."

Virgo
11 December 2025

Today Dear Virgo, creativity is your ally. Whether you're working on a personal project, solving a problem, or exploring new ideas, today's energy supports thinking outside the box. Don't hesitate to try new approaches or experiment with different methods. Your innovative thinking will lead to exciting breakthroughs and fresh opportunities. Trust in your ability to see things from a unique perspective and let your creativity guide you toward success.

Affirmation & Gratitude

"I embrace my creative spirit, allowing it to guide me toward new ideas and exciting possibilities."

Virgo
12 December 2025

Today Dear Virgo, communication is key to success. Whether you're resolving conflicts, having important conversations, or simply connecting with others, your ability to express yourself clearly and thoughtfully will lead to positive outcomes. Be open to listening to others and offering your perspective with empathy. Honest and open communication will build trust and strengthen your relationships. Don't shy away from important conversations—today is a great day for healing through dialogue. Approach conversations with kindness and clarity.

Affirmation & Gratitude

"I communicate openly and kindly, trusting that clarity and understanding lead to stronger connections and healing."

Virgo
13 December 2025

Today Dear Virgo, self-care is essential. You may feel the need to rest and recharge after a busy period. Take time to focus on your well-being, whether through physical rest, emotional nourishment, or simply taking time to slow down. Today's energy supports healing and renewal, so don't hesitate to take a break from your responsibilities. You'll return to your tasks feeling refreshed and ready to tackle what's ahead.

Affirmation & Gratitude

"I honor my body's need for rest and renewal, allowing myself to recharge and feel rejuvenated."

Virgo
14 December 2025

Today Dear Virgo, teamwork is emphasized. Whether you're collaborating with colleagues, friends, or family, today's energy supports cooperation and shared success. Be open to others' ideas and contributions, and don't hesitate to offer your insights. Together, you'll achieve greater results than you could alone. Trust in the power of teamwork and the value of collaboration. Embrace the support and contributions of those around you, and celebrate the joy of working together toward common goals.

Affirmation & Gratitude

"I am grateful for the power of teamwork, knowing that collaboration leads to shared success and deeper connections."

Virgo
15 December 2025

Today Dear Virgo, creativity flows easily. Whether you're working on a personal project, solving problems, or exploring new ideas, today's energy supports innovative thinking. Don't hesitate to experiment with different approaches or try something new. Your unique perspective will lead to exciting breakthroughs and fresh opportunities. Trust in your creative abilities, and let your imagination guide you toward success. Embrace the freedom of creative expression, and enjoy the process of discovery.

Affirmation & Gratitude

"I embrace my creative spirit, allowing it to guide me toward new ideas and exciting possibilities."

Virgo
16 December 2025

Today Dear Virgo, relationships take center stage. Whether you're connecting with family, friends, or a romantic partner, today's energy supports nurturing your bonds. Show appreciation for the people who bring joy and support to your life, and make an effort to strengthen your connections. Thoughtful gestures and meaningful conversations will deepen your relationships and create lasting bonds. Be fully present in your interactions, and your relationships will flourish.

Affirmation & Gratitude

"I nurture my relationships with love and care, knowing that strong connections bring joy and fulfillment."

Virgo

17 December 2025

Today Dear Virgo, balance is key to staying grounded. You may have a lot on your plate, but it's important to create harmony between work and personal obligations. Prioritize your tasks and make time for self-care. By maintaining balance, you'll feel more centered and capable of handling the day's demands with ease. Don't forget that your well-being is just as important as your productivity. Balance leads to both peace and success.

Affirmation & Gratitude

"I create balance in my life, knowing that harmony between work and rest leads to peace and fulfillment."

Virgo
18 December 2025

Today Dear Virgo, communication is highlighted. Whether you're resolving misunderstandings, having important conversations, or simply connecting with others, your ability to express yourself clearly and thoughtfully will lead to positive outcomes. Be open to listening to others and offering your insights with empathy. Today's energy supports healing and growth through dialogue, so don't hesitate to address unresolved issues. By fostering clear communication, you'll strengthen your relationships and build trust.

Affirmation & Gratitude

"I communicate openly and kindly, trusting that clarity and understanding lead to stronger connections and healing."

♍ Virgo

19 December 2025

Today Dear Virgo, creativity is your greatest ally. Whether you're working on a personal project, brainstorming new ideas, or finding solutions to challenges, today's energy supports thinking outside the box. Don't be afraid to try new approaches or experiment with different methods. Your innovative thinking will lead to breakthroughs and exciting opportunities. Trust in your ability to see things from a fresh perspective, and let your creative spirit guide you toward success.

Affirmation & Gratitude

"I embrace my creative spirit, allowing it to guide me toward new ideas and exciting possibilities."

Virgo
20 December 2025

Today Dear Virgo, relationships are in focus. Whether you're spending time with loved ones, reconnecting with friends, or strengthening a romantic bond, today's energy supports deepening your connections. Be present and attentive with those who matter most, and show appreciation for the joy and support they bring into your life. Meaningful conversations and thoughtful gestures will strengthen your relationships and bring harmony. Open your heart to love and understanding, and your relationships will grow even stronger.

Affirmation & Gratitude

"I nurture my relationships with love and care, knowing that strong connections bring joy and fulfillment."

Virgo
21 December 2025

Today Dear Virgo, balance is essential. You may feel pulled between work and personal responsibilities, but it's important to find harmony between the two. Focus on prioritizing your tasks and make sure to take time for yourself. By maintaining balance, you'll feel more grounded and capable of handling the day's challenges with ease. Take care of your well-being as much as your responsibilities, and you'll find that balance brings peace and fulfillment.

Affirmation & Gratitude

"I create balance in my life, knowing that harmony between work and rest leads to peace and fulfillment."

Virgo
22 December 2025

Today Dear Virgo, creativity is highlighted, making it an ideal day to explore new ideas or revisit personal projects. Whether you're tackling a creative challenge or finding fresh solutions, today's energy supports innovative thinking. Don't be afraid to think outside the box and try something different. Your imagination will lead you to exciting breakthroughs and opportunities. Trust in your creative instincts, and let them guide you toward new possibilities. Embrace the joy of creative expression and the discoveries that come with it.

Affirmation & Gratitude

"I embrace my creative spirit, allowing it to guide me toward new ideas and exciting possibilities."

Virgo
23 December 2025

Today Dear Virgo, communication is essential. Whether you're resolving a conflict, having an important conversation, or simply connecting with others, your ability to express yourself clearly and thoughtfully will lead to positive outcomes. Be open to listening to others and offering your perspective with kindness. Honest dialogue will strengthen your relationships and build trust. Today's energy supports healing through communication, so don't hesitate to address any unresolved issues. Approach every conversation with empathy and clarity.

Affirmation & Gratitude

"I communicate openly and kindly, trusting that clarity and understanding lead to stronger connections and healing."

Virgo
24 December 2025

Today Dear Virgo, self-care is important. You've been busy lately, and today's energy encourages you to take time for yourself. Whether through rest, relaxation, or emotional nourishment, prioritize your well-being today. By taking care of yourself, you'll restore your energy and feel more balanced. Don't underestimate the importance of self-care—it's a vital part of maintaining both productivity and happiness. Take time to nurture yourself today, and you'll feel renewed.

Affirmation & Gratitude

"I honor my body's need for rest and renewal, knowing that self-care is essential for my well-being."

Virgo

25 December 2025

Today Dear Virgo, relationships take center stage. It's a day for connecting with loved ones and expressing gratitude for the people who bring joy to your life. Whether through meaningful conversations, quality time, or thoughtful gestures, your efforts to nurture your relationships will be rewarding. Be present and engaged with those who matter most, and show appreciation for the love and support they offer. Today's energy supports deepening your connections and creating lasting bonds.

Affirmation & Gratitude

"I nurture my relationships with love and care, knowing that strong connections bring joy and fulfillment."

Virgo
26 December 2025

Today Dear Virgo, balance is key. Whether you're managing work responsibilities or personal obligations, it's important to find harmony in your day. Focus on prioritizing your tasks and make time for relaxation and self-care. By maintaining balance, you'll feel more centered and capable of handling the demands of the day. Trust that balance will lead to both productivity and peace. Take care of yourself, and everything will fall into place with ease.

Affirmation & Gratitude

"I create balance in my life, knowing that harmony between work and rest leads to peace and fulfillment."

Virgo

27 December 2025

Today Dear Virgo, creativity flows effortlessly. Whether you're working on a personal project, solving problems, or exploring new ideas, today's energy supports thinking outside the box. Don't hesitate to experiment with new approaches or try something different. Your unique perspective will lead to exciting breakthroughs and opportunities. Trust in your creative spirit and allow it to guide you toward success. Embrace the excitement of creative expression, and enjoy the journey of discovery.

Affirmation & Gratitude

"I embrace my creative spirit, allowing it to guide me toward new ideas and exciting possibilities."

Virgo
28 December 2025

Today Dear Virgo, relationships are in focus. Whether you're spending time with family, reconnecting with friends, or nurturing a romantic bond, today's energy supports love and harmony. Be present with those who matter most and show appreciation for the joy they bring into your life. Thoughtful conversations and meaningful gestures will deepen your relationships and create lasting bonds. Open your heart to love and connection, and your relationships will flourish.

Affirmation & Gratitude

"I nurture my relationships with love and care, knowing that strong connections bring joy and fulfillment."

Virgo
29 December 2025

Today Dear Virgo, communication is key. Whether you're having important conversations, resolving conflicts, or simply connecting with others, your ability to express yourself clearly and thoughtfully will lead to positive outcomes. Be open to listening to others and offering your insights with empathy. Honest and open communication will build trust and strengthen your relationships. Don't hesitate to address any misunderstandings—today is a great day for healing through dialogue.

Affirmation & Gratitude

"I communicate openly and kindly, trusting that clarity and understanding lead to stronger connections and healing."

Virgo

30 December 2025

Today Dear Virgo, balance is important. As the year comes to a close, focus on creating harmony between your responsibilities and your well-being. Reflect on what you've accomplished and what you want to carry forward into the new year. Today's energy encourages you to find balance between work and relaxation. By prioritizing both, you'll feel more prepared for the year ahead. Take care of yourself, and you'll be ready to embrace the opportunities to come.

Affirmation & Gratitude

"I create balance in my life, knowing that harmony between work and rest leads to peace and fulfillment."

 Virgo
31 December 2025

Today Dear Virgo, it's time to celebrate your achievements. As the year ends, reflect on the progress you've made and the challenges you've overcome. Today's energy supports self-reflection and gratitude, so take time to appreciate how far you've come. Set your intentions for the new year with confidence and optimism. By celebrating your successes and acknowledging your growth, you'll feel ready to embrace new opportunities in the year ahead. Trust in your ability to continue moving forward with strength and clarity.

Affirmation & Gratitude

"I celebrate my growth and set new intentions, trusting that each step forward brings me closer to my dreams."

www.ingramcontent.com/pod-product-compliance
Lightning Source LLC
Chambersburg PA
CBHW071948070526
44583CB00015B/1113